New Directions for
Adult and Continuing
Education

Jovita M. Ross-Gordon
Joellen E. Coryell
COEDITORS-IN-CHIEF

Ecojustice Adult Education: Theory and Practice in the Cultivation of the Cultural Commons

Audrey M. Dentith
Wendy Griswold
EDITORS

Number 153 • Spring 2017
Jossey-Bass
San Francisco

Ecojustice Adult Education: Theory and Practice in the Cultivation of the Cultural Commons
Audrey M. Dentith and Wendy Griswold (eds.)
New Directions for Adult and Continuing Education, no. 153

Coeditors-in-Chief: *Jovita M. Ross-Gordon and Joellen E. Coryell*

NEW DIRECTIONS FOR ADULT AND CONTINUING EDUCATION, (Print ISSN: 1052-2891; Online ISSN: 1536-0717), is published quarter
by Wiley Subscription Services, Inc., a Wiley Company, 111 River St., Hoboken, NJ 07030-5774 USA.
Postmaster: Send all address changes to NEW DIRECTIONS FOR ADULT AND CONTINUING EDUCATION, John Wiley & Sons Inc., C/O Th
Sheridan Press, PO Box 465, Hanover, PA 17331 USA.

Information for subscribers
NEW DIRECTIONS FOR ADULT AND CONTINUING EDUCATION is published in 4 issues per year. Institutional subscription prices for 201
are:
Print & Online: US$454 (US), US$507 (Canada & Mexico), US$554 (Rest of World), €363 (Europe), £285 (UK). Prices are exclusive of tax. Asia
Pacific GST, Canadian GST/HST and European VAT will be applied at the appropriate rates. For more information on current tax rates, pleas
go to www.wileyonlinelibrary.com/tax-vat. The price includes online access to the current and all online back-files to January 1st 2013, whe
available. For other pricing options, including access information and terms and conditions, please visit www.wileyonlinelibrary.com/access.

Delivery Terms and Legal Title
Where the subscription price includes print issues and delivery is to the recipient's address, delivery terms are **Delivered at Place (DAP**
the recipient is responsible for paying any import duty or taxes. Title to all issues transfers FOB our shipping point, freight prepaid. We wi
endeavour to fulfil claims for missing or damaged copies within six months of publication, within our reasonable discretion and subject t
availability.

Back issues: Single issues from current and recent volumes are available at the current single issue price from cs-journals@wiley.com.

Disclaimer
The Publisher and Editors cannot be held responsible for errors or any consequences arising from the use of information contained in this journa
the views and opinions expressed do not necessarily reflect those of the Publisher and Editors, neither does the publication of advertisemen
constitute any endorsement by the Publisher and Editors of the products advertised.

Publisher: NEW DIRECTIONS FOR ADULT AND CONTINUING EDUCATION is published by Wiley Periodicals, Inc., 350 Main St., Malde
MA 02148-5020.

Journal Customer Services: For ordering information, claims and any enquiry concerning your journal subscription please go t
www.wileycustomerhelp.com/ask or contact your nearest office.
Americas: Email: cs-journals@wiley.com; Tel: +1 781 388 8598 or +1 800 835 6770 (toll free in the USA & Canada).
Europe, Middle East and Africa: Email: cs-journals@wiley.com; Tel: +44 (0) 1865 778315.
Asia Pacific: Email: cs-journals@wiley.com; Tel: +65 6511 8000.
Japan: For Japanese speaking support, Email: cs-japan@wiley.com.
Visit our Online Customer Help available in 7 languages at www.wileycustomerhelp.com/ask

Production Editor: Poornita Jugran (email: pjugran@wiley.com).

Wiley's Corporate Citizenship initiative seeks to address the environmental, social, economic, and ethical challenges faced in our business an
which are important to our diverse stakeholder groups. Since launching the initiative, we have focused on sharing our content with those i
need, enhancing community philanthropy, reducing our carbon impact, creating global guidelines and best practices for paper use, establishir
a vendor code of ethics, and engaging our colleagues and other stakeholders in our efforts. Follow our progress at www.wiley.com/go/citizenshi

View this journal online at wileyonlinelibrary.com/journal/ace

Wiley is a founding member of the UN-backed HINARI, AGORA, and OARE initiatives. They are now collectively known as Research4Lif
making online scientific content available free or at nominal cost to researchers in developing countries. Please visit Wiley's Content Access
Corporate Citizenship site: http://www.wiley.com/WileyCDA/Section/id-390082.html

Printed in the USA by The Sheridan Group.
Address for Editorial Correspondence: Coeditors-in-Chief, *Jovita M. Ross-Gordon and Joellen E. Coryell,* NEW DIRECTIONS FOR ADULT AN
CONTINUING EDUCATION, Email: jross-gordon@txstate.edu

Abstracting and Indexing Services
The Journal is indexed by Academic Search Alumni Edition (EBSCO Publishing); ERIC: Educational Resources Information Center (CSC
Higher Education Abstracts (Claremont Graduate University); Sociological Abstracts (ProQuest).

Cover design: Wiley
Cover Images: © Lava 4 images | Shutterstock

For submission instructions, subscription and all other information visit:
wileyonlinelibrary.com/journal/ace

CONTENTS

Editors' Notes

No crisis is as great as the environmental predicament we face. Problems of extreme weather, waste disposal, pollution, overpopulation, and changes in the chemistry of the world's oceans now beset us. Changes in the natural ecologies of the world represent a decline in the quality of life for the majority of the world's people (Brown, 2008). Yet, market forces continue to promote a culture that fosters a dependency on consumerism in Western countries. Education has never been more important as it is today. The authors in this volume attest to this declaration and demonstrate the immense influence of education in the promotion of sustainable life through ecojustice philosophy.

The ecological crisis warrants our immediate attention as adult educators. In the field of adult education, we have been largely silent about the ecological/cultural crisis and the ways it will impact adult life and development in the years ahead, especially as droughts, shortages of water, sources of protein, and the computerization of jobs lead to even more economic uncertainties. The root causes of the ecological crisis and sustainability for the world's people are not widely discussed in adult education. Nor are the ways in which adults might meet the challenges being discussed in this volume. Today, as ecological issues increase and concern worldwide is mounting about the changing nature of work and cultural life, the field of adult education must respond to the educational needs of people, not corporations. It is imperative that we (re)educate adults about productive but sustainable work, stronger local community living, within an understanding of the relational being and the interdependency of all living and non-living things. That is, we need to find new ways of not only living lightly on the land but fundamentally changing our cultural understandings of everyday life.

Adult education holds much potential for its ability to highlight cultural knowledge, promote change, and maximize the capacity of adults to work together in strengthening mutually supportive communities that contribute to a sustainable future. No other field of education is more perfectly poised to address these needs or confront environmental issues than the field of adult education. Adult learning is more central to the societal reproduction, resistance and transformation of culture than the education of youth and children who lack in the depth of experience that will be required in the coming years. Resistance to and the transformation of societal structures emerge more vibrantly from the adult population. When men and women see the world in new ways, they engage with purpose and determination.

We all need to be open to community-centered alternatives to the money economy, and alternate ways of living productive lives. Ideas about intelligence and success that are more relational, ecologically situated, and less individualistic need to be discussed in adult education classrooms. New relationships that challenge our ideas about the role and practice of education might be

New Directions for Adult and Continuing Education, no. 153, Spring 2017 © 2017 Wiley Periodicals, Inc.
Published online in Wiley Online Library (wileyonlinelibrary.com) • DOI: 10.1002/ace.20216

forged among universities. Certainly, adult educators would be well-advised to study grassroots efforts in order to engage with the lived experience of adults who are engaged in the processes of cultural change.

In this edited collection, the cultural roots of the ecological/cultural crisis and its relationship to adult education have been explored. The development of sound practices and new cultural understandings among adults are emphasized. Certainly, there exists evidence of small grassroots work that generates hope as these build skills for the coming of a new age, an age of sustainable and just life. Chapter 1 provides an overview of the connections between sustainability, environmental and ecojustice education. Chapters 2 through 4 are focused on radical sustainability adult education, the branch of adult education most closely aligned with ecojustice. These chapters focus on established cultural institutions as potential agents of change. Chapter 6 discusses the principles of ecojustice education, while Chapters 6 through 8 share detailed examples of the implementation of those principles in formal and community education settings.

Audrey M. Dentith
Wendy Griswold
Editor's

Reference

Brown, L. R. (2008). *Plan B 3.0: Mobilizing to save civilization.* New York, NY: Norton.

AUDREY M. DENTITH, PhD, is a professor and director of the doctoral program at Appalachian State University in Boone, North Carolina. She teaches courses in environmental leadership, qualitative methods, and curriculum theory. She publishes in the area of ecojustice education, women's issues, and curriculum studies.

WENDY GRISWOLD, PhD, is an assistant professor in the Department of Leadership at the University of Memphis in Memphis, Tennessee. She teaches courses in global and comparative issues, community education, and adult learning. She publishes in the areas of sustainability education and participatory action research.

New Directions for Adult and Continuing Education • DOI: 10.1002/ace

1

Adult education has a significant role to play in creating a just and sustainable world. This chapter explores a continuum of perspectives related to the environment and education and highlights sustainability and ecojustice education theory and practices in this volume.

Sustainability, Ecojustice, and Adult Education

Wendy Griswold

Our environment and human impact upon it is a growing concern. Sustainability and sustainable development have been advanced as a response to this increasingly pressing global issue. The term *sustainable development* (World Commission on Environment, 1987) entered our vocabulary in the 1980s and has been contested, politically charged, and evolving ever since. Conceptions of sustainability have been delineated into two philosophical camps, radical and conservative. Radicals view sustainability as focused on environmental protection, equity, local knowledge, and the intersections of environmental, social, and economic issues. The conservative view is focused on environmental conservation, downplays the importance of equity, emphasizes expert knowledge, and views sustainability largely as an environmental problem, not an economic and social one (Jacobs, 1999). Regardless of one's philosophical view on sustainability, education is recognized as a key factor in moving toward sustainability.

The radical perspective on sustainability education is largely transformative in nature, while the conservative perspective is transmissive (Jickling & Wals, 2008). Within the field of adult education, sustainability is viewed from a more radical perspective. As the field of adult education expands, the inclusion of sustainability education under its umbrella can enhance the scholarly contributions to the research necessary for positive change.

Sustainability Overview

There is no singular definition or agreed-on meaning for the concept of sustainability (Jickling & Wals, 2008). One of the earliest and most widely accepted definitions of sustainability emerged from the Brundtland Commission: "sustainable development is development that meets the needs of the present

NEW DIRECTIONS FOR ADULT AND CONTINUING EDUCATION, no. 153, Spring 2017 © 2017 Wiley Periodicals, Inc.
Published online in Wiley Online Library (wileyonlinelibrary.com) • DOI: 10.1002/ace.20217

without compromising the ability of future generations to meet their own needs" (World Commission on Environment and Development, 1987, p. 43).

The major tension within sustainability discourse and practice is the tension between maintaining the status quo and changing our existing power structures and relationships. The contested issues center on four main concepts: environment, equity, participation, and quality of life (Jacobs, 1999). A conservative sustainability perspective views the environment solely as an unlimited resource for human consumption and only seeks to protect the environment as long as that protection does not impede economic growth. The more radical approaches to sustainability have a tendency toward deeper respect for the natural environment and thus seek to encourage stronger protections for its preservation. Equity is ignored or de-emphasized on the conservative platform, particularly in the northern hemisphere, creating tensions at the global level (e.g., Davenport, 2015). Toward the more radical stance, advocating resource redistribution and raising global living standards are key concerns. In this volume, we address educational sustainability in a focused way from the radical perspective as we advocate the creation of a new paradigm in human connection to the environment and to one another.

Sustainability Education Overview

McKeown (2006) views sustainability education as an evolution of environmental education, which involves "improving basic education, reorienting existing education to address sustainable development, developing public understanding and awareness, and training" (p. 15). Jaimie Cloud of the Cloud Institute for Sustainability Education defines it as "an education that prepares people to be far-seeing enough, flexible enough, and wise enough to contribute to the regenerative capacity of the physical and social systems upon which they depend" (Cloud Institute for Sustainability Education, 2009, p. 4). These differing definitions highlight the opposing philosophical viewpoints that underlie educational approaches and the overall discourse on sustainability itself.

Opposing perspectives exist in that in an anthropocentric perspective, human existence is paramount and the environment is viewed as a natural resource focused solely on humanity, whereas an ecocentric approach extends this concern to nonhuman species and views the environment as its own entity (Kopnina, 2012). The concepts of environmental and ecological justice are examples of the difference in perspectives. Environmental justice is "the distribution of environmental benefits and burdens among human beings" (Kopnina, 2012, p. 703). Ecological justice and ecojustice education are centrally about "justice between human beings and the rest of the natural world" (Low & Gleeson, 1988, as cited in Kopnina, 2012, p. 703).

In general, approaches used in sustainability education tend to be transmissive (shallow) or transformative (deeper). Transmissive education involves curricula created and controlled by a few and either re-creates the accepted social order or a new order determined by its creators (generally government and industry). In a transmissive approach to sustainability education, the environment is a problem to be solved (Stevenson, 2006). It also positions the environment, economics, and social issues as separate spheres, which places them in opposition to each other, and leads us to deal with them as problems within separate arenas instead of part of the same whole (Rathzel & Uzell, 2009). Transformative education is co-created knowledge that has been socially constructed by a broad base of participants and has the capacity to move us beyond sustainable development (Jickling & Wals, 2008). A transformative approach claims the focus on environmental problems doesn't allow for a healthy environment to be the norm and leads to oversimplification of environmental issues on the part of educators in their curricula (Stevenson, 2006). It also seeks to illuminate the interrelation among the environment, economics, and social issues (Rathzel & Uzell, 2009). Transmissive education, in a sustainability context, focuses on individual behaviors and concerns, consists of discrete facts about the environment, and relies on rational ways of knowing (Stevenson, 2006). Transformative curricula emphasizes community or society, places environmental concerns in the context of local issues, and incorporates emotions, values and spirituality as ways of knowing (Stevenson, 2006). Transformative approaches are heavily incorporated into ecojustice and radical sustainability adult education (Clover, 2003; Dentith & Thompson, Chapter 6, this volume; Walter, 2009).

Adult Education and Sustainability

In order to facilitate transformative learning and positive change, the field of adult education can serve as a catalyst for sustainability and ecojustice education. Tension between maintaining the status quo and creating social change is evident in both fields of adult education and sustainability education. Ostrom, Martin, and Zacharakis (2008) identified this tension as a "divide between those for whom adult education is a tool for social progress, and those who view it as a means for individual human development" (p. 306).

Radical environmental adult education has been influenced by the demand created through the sustainability movement (Walter, 2009). Clover (2003) outlined the common conceptual frameworks and strategies of radical environmental adult education, which include:

- making explicit the links between the environment, society, economics, politics, and culture;
- utilizing engaged and participatory learning process not limited to individual behavior change and information transmission;
- focusing on root causes and critical questioning of market/consumer driven capitalism and globalization; and
- learning that is community oriented and contextually shaped.

Within the sustainability and environmental adult education literature (a relatively small, but growing body of work), much of the scholarship is rooted in nonformal, informal, and community learning contexts (Bell & Clover, Chapter 2, this volume). An emerging perspective is ecojustice adult education, which incorporates many of the principles of radical environmental adult education, with a strong emphasis on the role of the cultural commons in restoring and sustaining healthy ecosystems. Two areas of theory and practice that inform ecojustice and radical environmental adult education are transformative and situated learning.

Transformative Learning. Transformative learning from a planetary perspective or ecological consciousness "recognizes the interconnectedness among universe, planet, natural environment, human community, and personal world. Most significant is recognizing the individual not just from a social-political dimension but also from an ecological and planetary one" (Taylor, 2008, pp. 9–10). Major tenets of ecological consciousness include relationships and reciprocity, especially concerning the co-creation of knowledge. The physical environment helps to shape and inform social constructs. In this volume (Chapter 6), Dentith and Thompson describe their work as indicative of transformational learning among adults engaged in a seminar on ecojustice education.

Recent research exploring sustainability adult education in a variety of contexts using the lens of transformative learning indicate an important role for instrumental learning (Moyer & Sinclair, 2016; Quinn & Sinclair, 2016; Sims & Sinclair, 2008). This holds true in ecojustice education, as well, given its emphasis on relearning the cultural skills that support sustainable ecosystems (Bowers, Chapter 5, this volume). Instrumental learning is about the technical and the rational, while communicative learning helps us understand and develop skills about human communication and make meaning of social experiences (Mezirow, 2003). Devising new ways of being in the world requires a certain amount of instrumental learning and behavioral change.

Situated Learning. Lave and Wegner (1991) explored situated learning in communities with an emphasis on engagement and relationship as the site of learning. Situated learning involves "the whole person rather than 'receiving' a body of factual knowledge about the world; an activity in and with the world, and on the view that agent, activity, and the world mutually constitute each other" (Lave & Wegner, 1991, p. 33). According to their theory of legitimate peripheral participation, participation (or engagement) in relation to "old-timers" is the process by which newcomers form their identities in respective communities of practice (Lave & Wegner, 1991). Learning communities can serve as sites for introducing newcomers into more encompassing communities of practice. The capacity of situated learning to facilitate social reconstruction is of particular relevance to ecojustice and sustainability education. Situated learning may be an appropriate tool for the creation of sustainable societies, where "old" ways of acting and thinking may be problematic. While new members of a community need to learn from the previous generation, they may also need to transform the perspectives and practices in their communities in order to develop a distinct identity focused on ecojustice and sustainability and move toward the future (Lave & Wegner, 1991). Situated learning in environmental adult education is detailed in the essays by Kearns Burke in Chapter 8 and Winfrey in Chapter 7. To address the current ecological crisis, communities of practice focused on facilitating learning utilize situated learning to connect those with cultural skills aligned with sustainable practices with those who want to learn them. One example is the Transition Movement, a grassroots effort to develop community resilience to contemporary challenges such as climate change and the economic crisis discussed by Kearns Burke in Chapter 8.

The research and practices described in this volume are examples of contributions to adult learning theory and ecojustice and sustainability adult education that reflect the potential impact adult education can make toward achieving global justice. There is much more to explore and learn as humanity prepares to undertake its most serious challenge yet.

Moving Toward (and Beyond) Sustainability Adult Education

The goal of radical/strong/deep sustainability and ecojustice adult education is to develop a citizenry capable of re-creating the world to ensure a healthy and equitable existence for all. Although this chapter has focused largely on sustainability education, the chapters ahead demonstrate the close alignment between radical sustainability adult education and ecojustice adult education. It is evident that both speak from the position that cultural change is necessary to address our ecological crisis. The current pervasive world view is not one in which environmental, social, or economic justice is possible. This volume contains examples of efforts to facilitate cultural change from both radical sustainability and ecojustice adult educators. Their examples provide guidance on how to facilitate adult learning free from prescribed outcomes, the type of learning necessary for recreating the world.

The first step in facilitating ecojustice or radical sustainability education is to clarify our worldviews about the environment and develop our own visions of what a sustainable society looks like (Stevenson, 2006). Then we need to consciously find ways to communicate our worldview and vision through our teaching. Chet Bowers (Chapter 5, this volume) highlights how our language reveals and frames our values and world views. If our language is devoid of words that convey respect and connection to nature, what does that communicate about our worldview?

Once we have clarified our own perspectives and visions, we can create space for our learners to do the same. We can begin by simply making space in our curricula for exploring the connections between ourselves and the environment. Many chapters in this volume detail the authors' experiences with this process. Groen's essay on the role of spirituality in cultivating ecological consciousness offers an internal and personal view of this journey. Making space in our curricula requires us to reflect critically on our own teaching and look for opportunities to help our learners critically reflect their role in contributing to our current situation and develop new perspectives to "help ameliorate the crisis and live sustainable lives" (Dentith & Thompson, Chapter 6, this volume). These opportunities need to be rooted in local issues of relevance and concern to learners. As we well know:

> Adults tend to be more motivated to learn and to act by things they care about rather than by abstract concerns, and one critical role of educators is to show people why they should care about the environment before expecting them to acknowledge its importance and begin to build environmental literacy. (St. Clair, 2003, p. 74)

In their chapter on teaching ecojustice education, Dentith and Thompson provide a concrete example of facilitating student caring and connection to content. For too long, the ecological dimension has been missing from learning and education. We are disconnected from the fact that we are dependent on the earth for our own survival. The job of sustainability, ecojustice adult education, and environmental adult education is to address this deficiency. In fact, any adult educator concerned about or working in the areas of social and/or economic justice must broaden their theory and practice to include the environment. These issues are too inextricably linked to address piecemeal. Our attitudes and worldviews toward the environment are bound up in our current system, which perpetuates the injustice we seek to end. If we stubbornly continue this disconnect, our efforts toward justice will fail in the long term.

This volume is an introduction to the theory and practice of adult education intended to support the development of sustainable cultures. Two branches of this type of adult education are discussed: radical sustainability or environmental education and ecojustice education. Radical sustainability and environmental adult education have been emerging over the past few decades. The ecojustice perspective in adult education is even more nascent. The chapters in this volume highlight theory and practice in each respective sphere of inquiry. The common threads uniting them are the linkages between environmental, social, and economic issues; an insistence that the relationship between nature and humanity must change; and the role of adult education in facilitating this change.

There are three chapters that can be categorized as radical sustainability adult education. Each focuses on established cultural institutions as change agents. Janet Groen details her experience of cultivating ecological awareness during a Jesuit retreat focused on eco-spirituality. She describes how the tradition of the Ignatian Spiritual Exercises, originally developed by St. Ignatius to help deepen one's relationship with God, has been expanded to "emphasize our connection to nature and the underlying reasons for our ecological crisis" (Groen, Chapter 3, this volume). Key elements of the practice is for participants to come to terms with their roles in the current crisis and to develop a future vision. Lorraine Bell and Darlene Clover discuss the role of museums as facilitators of public dialog and exploration of environmental issues. Rather than reflecting and reinforcing existing perspectives about the relationship of humans and the environment, their work points to how public cultural institutions can challenge this relationship. Key elements are making space for critical questioning to occur and for other ways of knowing to emerge in public spaces. Catherine Etmanski and Ingrid Kajzer-Mitchell explore how one of the world's oldest professions serves as a catalyst for transforming consumers into activists and learners. Their case study demonstrates the roles of small scale farmers as educators and leaders in cultivating change in food systems. Key elements are informal, self-directed, and action learning.

Although the chapters on radical sustainability education provide examples of cultural institutions as change agents, the chapters on ecojustice education are directly embedded in community efforts. Bowers describes the principles of ecojustice education and introduces the concept of the cultural commons, a key concept in the area of adult ecojustice education. The cultural commons include "non-monetized and non-privately owned knowledge, skills and mentoring relationships that have been handed down over the generations" (Bowers, Chapter 5, this volume). An ecojustice adult education perspective asserts that redirecting humanity's focus to the cultural commons will produce the cultural perspective shift needed to alter our current course. In their chapter, Dentith and Thompson provide a practical example of putting the principles of ecojustice adult education into action within the context of formal educational settings. They describe a workshop for educational leaders designed to help them identify their role in the current environmental crisis and devise ways they could facilitate change in their personal and professional lives. Emily Kearns Burke provides an example of community efforts to revitalize the cultural commons in her chapter on the Transition Movement. The Transition Movement is a grassroots initiative that is responding to the current environmental crisis by fostering community resilience efforts, seeking to teach the skills of the cultural commons to address food and energy issues. Key elements are the use of situated learning, mentoring, and cognitive apprenticeships to connect intergenerational learners in teaching and learning. Nancy Winfrey provides a second example of grassroots initiatives to promote ecojustice education in her study of the Pittsboro Plenty, an initiative to launch a community currency system. Through the use of local currency systems, control of the economic development is retained at the community level. Key elements in creating successful systems include participatory decision-making processes, human rights, social justice, and sustainability.

Conclusion

This volume offers a path forward for adult educators concerned with facilitating the conditions within which justice can emerge. Adult education has a significant role to play in creating a just and sustainable world. Every adult educator has a worldview that includes perspectives, attitudes, and values about the environment and education. These worldviews fall somewhere along the continuums described earlier. Responsible practitioners will engage in critical reflection to uncover and make explicit their assumptions about the environment and their role as educators in the movement beyond sustainability.

References

Cloud Institute for Sustainability Education. (2009). *What is education for sustainability (EfS)?* Retrieved from http://cloudinstitute.org/our-approach/

Clover, D. E. (2003). Environmental adult education: Critique and creativity in a globalizing world. In D. Clover & L. Hill (Eds.), *New directions for adult and continuing education, 99. Special issue: Environmental adult education: Ecological learning, theory, and practice for socioenvironmental change* (pp. 5–15). New York, NY: Wiley.

Davenport, C. (2015, December 12). Nations approve landmark climate accord in Paris. *The New York Times.* Retrieved from http://www.nytimes.com/2015/12/13/world/europe/climate-change-accord-paris.html?_r=0

Jacobs, M. (1999). Sustainable development as a contested concept. In A. Dobson (Ed.), *Fairness and futurity: Essays on environmental sustainability and social justice* (pp. 21–45). New York, NY: Oxford University Press.

Jickling, B., & Wals, A. E. J. (2008). Globalization and environmental education: Looking beyond sustainable development. *Journal of Curriculum Studies, 40*(1), 1–21.

Kopnina, H. (2012). Education for sustainable development (ESD): The turn away from "environment" in environmental education? *Environmental Education Research, 18*(5), 699–717.

Lave, J., & Wegner, E. (1991). *Situated learning: Legitimate peripheral participation.* Cambridge, UK: Cambridge University Press.

McKeown, R. (2006). Education for sustainable development toolkit, United Nations Educational, Scientific, and Cultural Organization, Paris. Retrieved from www.unesco.org/education/desd

Mezirow, J. (2003). Transformative learning as discourse. *Journal of Transformative Education, 1*, 58–63.

Moyer, J. M., & Sinclair, A. J. (2016). Stoking the dialog on the domains of transformative learning theory: Insights from research with faith-based organizations in Kenya. *Adult Education Quarterly, 66*(1), 39–56.

Ostrom, C. S., Martin, W. J., & Zacharakis, J. (2008). Autopoiesis and the cosmology of postmodern adult education. *Adult Education Quarterly, 58*(4), 299–317.

Quinn, L. J., & Sinclair, A. J. (2016). Undressing transformative learning: The roles of instrumental and communicative learning in the shift to clothing sustainability. *Adult Education Quarterly, 66*(3), 1–20.

Rathzel, N., & Uzzell, D. (2009). Transformative environmental education: A collective rehearsal for reality. *Environmental Education Research, 15*(3), 263–277.

Sims, L., & Sinclair, A. J. (2008). Learning through participatory resource management programs: Case studies from Costa Rica. *Adult Education Quarterly, 58*(2), 151–168.

St. Clair, R. (2003). Words for the world: Creating critical environmental literacy for adults. In D. Clover & L. Hill (Eds.), *New directions for adult and continuing education, 99. Special issue: Environmental adult education: Ecological learning, theory, and practice for socioenvironmental change* (pp. 69–78). New York, NY: Wiley.

Stevenson, R. B. (2006). Tensions and transitions in policy discourse: Recontextualising a decontextualised EE/ESD debate. *Environmental Education Research, 12*(3–4), 277–290.

Taylor, E. W. (2008). Transformative learning theory. In S.B. Merriam (Ed.), *New directions for adult and continuing education. Special issue: Third update on adult learning theory, 119* (pp. 5–15). Hoboken, NJ: Wiley.

Walter, P. (2009). Philosophies of adult environmental education. *Adult Education Quarterly*, 60(1), 3–25.

World Commission on Environment and Development. (1987). *Our common future*. Oxford, UK: Oxford University Press.

WENDY GRISWOLD *is an assistant professor in the Department of Leadership at the University of Memphis in Memphis, Tennessee.*

2

This chapter explores how museums, as educational and cultural institutions, can become agents of socioecological transformation. The ideas of critical museum studies and environmental adult education are reviewed, and three examples of environmental adult education in museums are discussed.

Critical Culture: Environmental Adult Education in Public Museums

Lorraine Bell, Darlene E. Clover

This chapter discusses the challenges and potentials of public museums (including galleries) as sites of environmental adult education. Adult educators have discussed how these cultural organizations have recently taken up complex social problems including racism, poverty, "othering," religious intolerance, homophobia, and neighborhood gentrification (Clover, 2015; Fitchett, Merriweather, & Coffey, 2015; Frost, 2013; Gray, in press; Steedman, 2012; Szekeres, 2012), but less attention has been paid to how museums are tackling difficult and environmental problems such as climate change and our globalized food system. Yet Canadian museum scholar Janes (2008) suggests they are well positioned to address "the meaning and implications of our excessive consumption and deteriorating environment" (p. 23) and he calls on these public pedagogical institutions to become agents of change.

Along a similar trajectory, environmental adult educators have argued that we need more public spaces to examine the underlying economic and political ideologies and practices that have brought us near the brink of environmental collapse. These educators call for critical, creative, and participatory practices that challenge, for example, propagandist discourses of "ethical oil" the negation of climate change, and the profit at any cost mentality threatening the planet (Clover, Hall, & Follen, 2013).

We begin this chapter by acknowledging museums as important yet problematic pedagogical and cultural institutions, and explore recent critiques of their "legacies of elitism, paternalism and social exclusion" (Butler & Lehrer, 2016, p. 13). We then briefly review some key premises of environmental adult education in relation to these unique pedagogical spaces. We then share two examples from small museums in our home province of British Columbia, Canada and one from the Tate Modern in London, United Kingdom. These

NEW DIRECTIONS FOR ADULT AND CONTINUING EDUCATION, no. 153, Spring 2017 © 2017 Wiley Periodicals, Inc.
Published online in Wiley Online Library (wileyonlinelibrary.com) • DOI: 10.1002/ace.20218

examples, highlighting a community food activism project, facilitated conversations around controversial energy projects, and an environmental adult education program, show how museums and galleries of various sizes and situations can be involved with environmental adult education. We conclude that museums can challenge, rather than reinforce, dominant cultural narratives around the environment, and encourage reflection and dialogue. With their resources of visual, material, and intangible culture, public and accessible spaces, and fundamentally educational mandates, these public institutions can play a key role in the struggle for socioecological justice and transformation.

(Re)positioning Museums: Their Challenges and Potentials

Public museums are ubiquitous features of both rural and urban communities and are integral to our social, cultural, political, aesthetic, and educational infrastructures. Although we tend to think of their primary function as the collection and conservation of material culture, public museums have also been positioned as spaces for "informal individual learning as well as structured learning activities for groups" (UNESCO, 1999, pp. 3–4; see also Taylor, McKinley-Parrish, & Banz, 2010). But UNESCO's description leaves a question unanswered: education for whom and for what? Museums have a role in the shaping of knowledge, argues Hooper-Greenhill (1992) and through their collections and displays reflect and reinforce dominant ideologies and values. Canadian adult educator Scott (1998) further cautions that "the ability to articulate one's cognitive framework in regard to adult education is essential; otherwise we become vulnerable as we attempt to make change" (p. 106). This caveat is crucial when considering the role of these institutions as pedagogical agents of socioecological change.

We are in an era defined by Reinsborough (2010, p. 69) as a "slow motion apocalypse," and in which commentators such as Klein (2014) lament the cultural primacy of economic imperatives that view the environment as merely a source for materials and a sink for wastes. There are dominant values in society, she argues, which are "intimately tied to triumphant capitalism" (p. 52) and which are directly implicated in negative attitudes toward the environment. Thus, "the culture that triumphed in our corporate age pits us against the natural world" (p. 58). These ideological beliefs around resource extraction are further intensified in the neoliberal excesses of global capitalism, characterized by extensive deregulation and the polarization of power and wealth. The role of social movements, she argues "is not to accept dominant values as fixed and unchangeable but to offer other ways to live-to wage, and win, a battle of cultural worldviews . . . " (p. 59). She argues that part of this struggle means

> . . . continually drawing connections among seemingly disparate struggles . . . that the logic that would cut pensions, food stamps, and health care

New Directions for Adult and Continuing Education • DOI: 10.1002/ace

before increasing taxes on the rich is the same logic that would blast the bedrock of the earth to get the last vapors of gas and the last drops of oil before making the shift to renewable energy. (p. 59)

Within this milieu, public cultural institutions have been called on, in their curatorial, adult education and community outreach practices, to encourage dialogue and cultural democracy (e.g., see Abram, 2005; Ashley, 2006; Casey, 2007; Janes, 2008; McTavish, 2003; Sandell & Nightingale, 2012; Watson, 2007). A challenge to this movement is that governments and other funders tend to encourage pragmatic and politically expedient initiatives rather than the deep, analytical activities required for change (Thompson, 2002).

These institutions also struggle with a legacy of elitism, patriarchy, colonialism, sexism, and exclusivity, all of which tend to legitimate existing social relations of power (e.g., Borg & Mayo, 2010; Mayo, 2013; Onciul, 2015; Phillips, 2011). A further complication is that education in these institutions has often been de-emphasized and underfunded (e.g., M.C. Chobot & Chobot, 1990; Clover, 2015; Ellis, 2002). The result is that museums are rarely considered in discussions around environmental issues such as climate change, air and water pollution, food and housing security, and the collapse of natural resources. Janes (2008) argues that we should expect more from public institutions whose primary mandate is knowledge and learning, and that museums must instead offer an "intellectual and civic resource in times of profound social and environmental change" (p. 23).

A key challenge for museums today, according to Ashley (2005), is to overcome their conformity to singular historical narratives and their relentlessly uncritical celebration of nationalism, colonialism, and industrialism. In a manner decidedly unhelpful to addressing our collective socioecological crises, museums have purveyed authoritative and uncritical views of economic and resource development through what Ashley describes as their "muscular narratives of nation building" (p. 6). Here, Ashley notes modern capitalist development becomes entangled with emotive evocations of nationalism and cultural identity. These narratives, "closely wrapped up in nineteenth century efforts to define nations" (p. 6; see also Anderson, 1983; Bennett, 1995) have equated industrial development with "technological advance and the subordination of nature to humanity" (MacDonald & Alsford, 1995, p. 278) and with "the dominant culture's economic and political interests" (Ashley, 2005, p. 6). While appearing neutral, these narratives present unchallenged characterizations of urbanization, industrial mining, logging, fishing, and other forms of resource based industry as "heroic," "pioneering," "settling," and "nation-building." They leave unquestioned the cultural, social, and environmental havoc created by particular modes of development. Unpacking how museums "shape the ways in which information and symbolic content are produced and circulated in society" (Ashley, 2005, p. 5) involves the recognition of the cultural values that shape the relationship between the environment and humanity that are silently embedded in these narratives.

Although it is clear that museums *are* changing in response to evolving ideas around their social and pedagogical roles, *how* they change, and whether there will be space/s for the critical environmental adult education approaches that are discussed elsewhere in this book, remains to be seen. Some museum-based adult educators have recently taken up the challenge to develop what Clover and Stone (in press) refer to as a "critical cultural aesthetic" and have sought to engage with their communities in learning, dialogue and action toward socioecological change. These environmentally themed exhibitions, displays, activities, and programs contribute to the discourse of environmental adult education by emphasizing collectivity, creativity, and epistemological diversity. Our current task as environmental adult educators is to find ways to collaborate with museum professionals in developing critical and creative pedagogies that recognize and compliment the unique pedagogical resources of museums. In the following section, we review some key ideas found in environmental adult education and discuss their relevance to museums.

Environmental Adult Education and Museums

"Archives of the Commons" Link the Social and Ecological. Environmental adult educators such as Clover et al. (2013) and critical place based educators such as Gruenewald (2008) suggest that consideration for ecological systems from local to global, and our place within them, should permeate all forms of education. They suggest that a key pedagogical challenge for adult educators is to challenge the false bifurcation of social/ecological in both analysis and action. Formal and nonformal adult education, these educators argue, should involve the critical challenge of "ideological systems and societal structures that hinder and impede human development and socioenvironmental change" (Welton, 1995, p. 13), and nurture alternative knowledge(s) (e.g., Borg & Mayo, 2010).

As social and pedagogical institutions, museums have aesthetic, cultural, and civic resources, as well as publicly accessible spaces in which adult learners can engage with new and sometimes uncomfortable ideas. In addition, museums are often deeply embedded in their regions and communities, and have long been concerned with the preservation of local knowledge(s) and experience. They can, conceivably, expand on these functions to develop programs where adults can learn about the sociocultural basis of the ecological crisis through the exploration of situated knowledge(s). Community museums in particular have a unique capacity for documenting, preserving, and sharing individual and community life experiences. Barr (in press) suggests that when viewing museums in this light, "culture becomes a primary means for visualizing alternatives ... an active, historical agent involved in creative questioning and dissent" (n.p.). This is an important insight for adult pedagogies that seek to encourage what Dentith (this volume) describes as "community traditions

New Directions for Adult and Continuing Education • DOI: 10.1002/ace

around self-sufficiency" and ecological sustainability. Reimagining museums as "archives of the commons" also presents an alternative to the prevalent belief that the environmental crisis can be solved by scientific inquiry alone, or technological progress paired with rationalist, liberal discourse. Instead, it places renewed attention and value on local knowledge and traditions, imbued with experience and embedded in both time and place.

Collective Problems Require Critical Cultural Spaces for Collective Learning. As environmental adult educators, we feel that a socioecological approach to adult education has been neglected in favor of a heavy emphasis on career training and individual development. This approach to adult education tends to position the environmental crisis as a concern of scientists and specialized professions, rather than as a challenge for all people and communities. Clover et al. (2013) argue that

> ... as adult educators we must work to enhance people's collective potential to learn, ... and to help them more fully realize their capacities as ecological citizens. What people require are opportunities to reflect collectively upon the root causes of environmental problems, and not simply to respond individually to what often appears on the surface. (p. 3)

As public institutions, museums can be important sites of collective inquiry because they are accessible to a wide spectrum of visitors regardless of age, ethnicity, profession, class, or gender. Increasingly one hears museum directors such as Chantal Pontbriand, of the new Museum of Contemporary Canadian Art, suggesting that museums are no longer the "official keepers of the culture" but are instead "today's Agora, a place where people come together and think together" (Whyte, 2015). Museums have also been theorized as "third spaces": informal public gathering places that are neither home nor work, and that are essential to local democracy and community vitality (California Association of Museums, 2012).

Science Alone Cannot Solve Environmental Problems. Another premise of environmental adult education is that while science helps us understand environmental problems, it cannot alone address their political, ideological, and sociocultural dimensions. Often, an onslaught of expert-driven scientific information "can be disempowering and fatiguing [and] problematically promote the belief that community members have no knowledge to offer and therefore, will not be able to address environmental problems without the proper 'facts'" (Clover et al., 2013, p. 4). Environmental adult educators seek to develop processes that are "engaging and creative" and that address the importance of alternative knowledge(s). These educational methods and approaches include collective arts, place, and experientially based learning such as storytelling, arts and crafts, music, place explorations, and much more, all of which are well-suited to the learning spaces of public museums.

New Directions for Adult and Continuing Education • DOI: 10.1002/ace

Environmental Adult Education in Museums

We turn now to examples of how museums, as "modern agora" or "third spaces," are addressing "the meaning and implications of our excessive consumption and deteriorating environment" (Janes, 2008, p. 23). Our aim is to illustrate how museum displays and programs can challenge, rather than reinforce, dominant socioecological narratives, and encourage much needed reflection and dialogue around contemporary environmental issues. These examples also show that this critically important public pedagogy can happen in museums of any size and with limited resources. What we have learned from museum educators worldwide are that what matters most is the belief that museums can be agents of socioecological change. A clear mandate, vision and training around critical adult education (e.g., Abram, 2005) is also helpful, as is the willingness to reach out to communities in new ways.

"A Very Organic Progression": Food Programs at the Parksville Museum. Environmental adult education seeks to reconnect with cultural practices that support sustainability, and that rediscover and nurture the cultural and civil commons. In her adult education work around food pedagogy, Sumner (2012) suggests that local food systems have been undermined by globalization and corporatized food systems. The result has been epidemics of both hunger and obesity, soil erosion and pollution, and widespread food insecurity of global proportions. Sumner calls for a return to viewing food not as a commodity but as a life good. The parameters of an alternative food system, she suggests, will have to return to "life values, centered on the civil commons and anchored by social justice" (Sumner, 2012, p. 63). The aim of this system would be "to ensure that everyone is fed nutritious food within the ecological limits of the planet" (Sumner, 2012, p. 63).

Learning to see food as a life good, and food systems as a part of the civil and cultural commons, requires a place to relearn and share knowledge and skills, and to create new relationships based on mutual support. One example of this is the unconventional yet popular food programs of the Parksville Museum, located on Vancouver Island, Canada. Starting with an idea from a board member who was strongly interested in the issue of food security, the museum started a weekly farmers market on its sizeable grounds. The museum staff and volunteers saw it as an opportunity to move away from the idea that their museum is a "static organization that just stores and displays artefacts" and toward being "community responsive and community driven" (Gervais, personal communication, June 13, 2016).

While the Farmer's Market started mainly as an event to draw in a new audience (Gervais, personal communication, June 13, 2016), the museum staff and volunteers began to learn more deeply about food issues, and further developed the program in response to what they learned was a silently peaking food crisis with both ecological and social dimensions. The museum is now part of a region wide movement to reinvigorate local food systems, providing

New Directions for Adult and Continuing Education • DOI: 10.1002/ace

a platform for local knowledge about food production that is "cemented in history" (Gervais, personal communication, June 13, 2016).

The programs highlight how strong food production once was on the island and how near self-sufficiency in food production has eroded over time. The globalization and industrialization of the food system discussed by Sumner (2012) has resulted in a situation of food insecurity, especially noteworthy on an island where vulnerable supplies rely heavily on the transportation of imports.

Adult educators and local experts, including a well-known master gardener from a local college and members of a local Farmer's Institute, joined vendors, buyers, and artisans to become part of a wider, collective goal toward developing a "common sense of food security" in the community. In addition, recently changed bylaws in the local municipality enabled smaller producers such as home gardeners as well as larger farms to participate.

Oriented toward adult learners, as "they are the ones most interested in food security," the programs have become "a rocket under our belts, and we have had to run to keep up" explains the museum's curator. Thus, the weekly Farmer's Market soon expanded into an Urban Farm School and Master Gardening classes, as well as an artisans market and learning programs around traditional skills such as blacksmithing, weaving, and pottery. The idea was to "take art back to its roots" and "challenge our contemporary view of the things we take for granted" (Gervais, personal communication, June 13, 2016).

The program relates to the mandate and resources of the museum by providing an historic lens to a contemporary problem. As the curator suggests, "you cannot know where you are going if you don't know where you've been." In this case, a popular public program not only attracts visitors but also facilitates the understanding and addressing of an important environmental issue: the erosion of the food and agricultural commons. The food program at the museum has also provided "an amazing platform for many conversations" (Gervais, personal communication, June 13, 2016) of interrelated environmental issues, such as the destruction of the kelp beds on which local herring runs depend. The heavily local theme is meant not only for local people but also for visitors. The goal is to help people become more interested in discovering "local alternatives wherever they live" and to do their own research on food production.

Kitimat Questions: Energy. Since 2012, the small coastal community of Kitimat, British Columbia, became a central focus of wider energy debates in Canada. The town is located at the terminus of a controversial major pipeline, the Enbridge Northern Gateway Project, which is designed to carry 525,000 barrels of diluted bitumen per day from the oil sands of Alberta across Rocky and Coast mountain ranges, salmon spawning rivers and Indigenous territories of British Columbia (Morton, 2015). From there, the "fuel would be loaded onto tankers and shipped through the Douglas Channel, a passage that narrows to less than a kilometer" (Morton, 2015). Other plans include several liquefied natural gas (LNG) pipelines, terminal, and shipping facilities;

an expansion of an existing aluminum smelter (District of Kitimat, 2016); and what would be one of the world's largest oil refineries (Hunter, 2013). The projects have been met with intense resistance from communities all over British Columbia and beyond over concerns about potential spills that could impact fisheries and wildlife habitat (Morton, 2015).

Inspired by ideas that museums can be agents of change, as well as the uncertainty and concerns that were emerging from the community about these oil and gas developments, the Kitimat Museum's staff saw it as an opportunity to "be mindful and relevant in this critical global time" (Avery, 2015, p. 19). According to Avery, "it felt like the right time to create an exhibition that provided a space for critical thinking about the energy debates" (Avery, 2015, p. 19). The exhibition included panels that explored energy production, type, and use, as well as hands-on displays on loan from the Canadian Science and Technology Museum. It also called on local citizens to contribute artwork that would be displayed among the information panels (Avery, 2015). Another important aspect of the exhibition was to gather public input in the form of questions about energy production, type, and use, as well as issues that surround a global energy future (e.g., Figures 2.1 and 2.2) to be presented to key stakeholders in government and industry. The questions were grouped into several thematic categories including economy, sustainability, consultation, activism, environment, innovation, regulation, risk, and history. Not offering any answers, the exhibition posed the question: given that energy is a critical world need, "what *are* the answers and what is possible?" (Kitimat Museum, 2016, para. 1). Related programming included a creative writing contest with high school students, public meetings, and invited speakers. Curators had received advice that "engaging adults in museum learning depends on how well the material is arranged in a storyline-short bits of information-with lots of audio visual stimulation-experiential-smell, too" (Avery, personal communication, June 3, 2016).

Although groundbreaking in its approach to public engagement, the curator had some critical reflections about this exhibition and its related adult education programming. She noted that adults can experience fatigue about environmental topics, and that many local residents expressed feeling overwhelmed by public hearings about pipelines and energy. Others suggested that the topic lacked relevance to their own lives, in spite of the number and magnitude of the proposed developments planned for their community. This underscores the goals of environmental adult educators to design educational projects that help elucidate the relationship between our own lives and environmental health and justice, and with approaches that enliven and inspire rather than overwhelm and alienate. Avery (2015, p. 19) also wonders if the public's expectation of museums as places of leisure and entertainment is an obstacle to facilitating learning and debate around critical issues. For patrons used to finding local history, culture, and artworks in the museum, she suggests, the presentation of a local issue was seen as nontraditional and controversial.

New Directions for Adult and Continuing Education • DOI: 10.1002/ace

Figure 2.1. Kitimat Questions: Energy

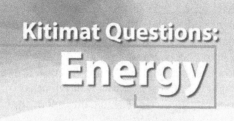

Kitimat Questions:

Energy

August 29 – October 18, 2014
Kitimat Museum & Archives

There are words that are frequently used when discussing energy. Given that energy is a most critical world need, and given that Kitimat has become the focus as a gateway to the Asia Pacific customer, the Kitimat Museum & Archives presents some thoughts and activities on the topic of energy.

Residents Submitted Questions

Well-used words in energy discussion have been chosen to group the questions. Social media and a focus group were vehicles for gathering resident's questions. These questions will be sent to key stakeholders and energy proponents in the private and public sectors, and will be published alongside responses in Kitimat Questions: Energy – our second exhibition opening in fall 2015.

Curator: Louise Avery
Co-Curator: Robin Rowland

Figure 2.2. Kitimat Asks

Kitimat Asks:

Q How does culture figure into decisions made on energy?

Q What is being done to relate to everyone's culture?

Q Does Alberta try to understand BC coastal culture?

Q Are aboriginal and non-aboriginal cultures in BC coming closer together or getting farther apart?

Art and Slow Violence. The Public Programs team at Tate Modern in London, United Kingdom, brings adults together for collaborative learning and reflection on art and society. *Art and Slow Violence* was a 5-week course that revolved around art displays of war, conflict, violence, and landscape. "Slow violence" describes the unequal impacts on the poor and women of climate change, deforestation, the acidification of oceans, oil spills, and the calamitous aftereffects of war.

The course was open to anyone interested in exploring the relationship between art and politics, and was well attended by participants with diverse backgrounds and interests. Participants spent time in the gallery spaces and engaged with video and photographic works by Omer Fast, Leon Golub, and Hrair Sarkissian. They also had quiet time outside of museum hours to sit among the artworks, and opportunities for informal gatherings and discussions.

Themes were generated whilst rendering visible what Mayo (2013) refers to as the "hidden codifications" of artworks, which helped participants make connections and develop critical thinking. For example, at Tate Britain, participants were introduced to two deceptively simple artworks in the permanent collection. One was a windy and chaotic landscape, a commons, where people collectively gathered food and fuel; the other, an estate mansion surrounded by an enclosed, heavily controlled and manicured garden "devoid" of humans. Manifest in the first work was the right to land, and the health and abundance of nature, while the latter illustrated the massive implications of the enclosures, which were enacted ideologies of privatization and social and ecological control. The participants carried these images to the contemporary exhibition, *Conflict, Time, Photography*. Many of these photographs showed landscapes in Iraq vacant of human activity and life, rendering visible the presence of ideology and its impact on the land and human lives.

The learning program at the Tate was reminiscent of Newman's (2006) calls for processes to connect ideology and reality, that destabilize and challenge things taken at face value, and that render visible the invisible hand of power and complicity. It highlighted the unique role of the aesthetic, which, argues Boal (2006), "enable[s] us to attain the truest and most profound comprehension of the world and society" (p. 29). Art can share creative insights that fill gaps in knowledge, and complete schemas, such as slow violence, which are often only "half-sensed" (Newman, 2006, p. 176). As we would expect of critical pedagogy in and of a complex world, the artworks suggest ways of seeing but offer no "correct" answers, leaving participants to ask themselves the difficult questions.

Too few spaces exist where people can actually engage in difficult conversations about these complex issues, and be exposed to theories and ideologies beyond their comfort zones. This course illustrated that art galleries can offer representational spaces that arouse epistemological curiosity and that pose new questions about the world and challenge the taken-for-granted.

New Directions for Adult and Continuing Education • DOI: 10.1002/ace

Conclusion

These examples show how museums as sites of critical and environmental adult education can challenge dominant narratives around socioecological issues through a cultural lens. They embrace collaborative and participatory approaches that encourage society-wide reflection and dialogue and apply a uniquely aesthetic and historical lens to contemporary problems. A complicating factor is what some view as the simultaneous "critique and commodification of museums" (McTavish, 2003, p. 107). An increasing "emphasis on profits, superficial blockbuster exhibitions, and the reduction of visitors to paying customers" (McTavish, 2003, p. 107; see also Janes, 2008) has led to a certain degree of ideological and professional tension in the field regarding the appropriate role and function of museums. We thus suggest that in order to be agents of socioecological change, these institutions must address their conservative traditions and singular narratives, and yet also be vigilant of current trends toward the commodification of heritage and culture. These examples show some ways in which museum educators and curators can develop provocative, radical, and imaginative education activities that can play an important role in the struggle for social and environmental change.

References

Abram, R. J. (2005). History is as history does: The evolution of a mission-driven museum. In R. R. Janes & G. T. Conaty (Eds.), *Looking reality in the eye: Museums and social responsibility* (pp.19–42). Calgary, AB: University of Calgary Press.

Anderson, B. (1983). *Imagined communities: Reflections on the origins and spread of nationalism.* New York, NY: Verso.

Ashley, S. (2005). State authority and the public sphere: Ideas on the changing role of the museum as a Canadian social institution. *Museum and Society*, 3(1), 5–17.

Ashley, S. L. (2006). Heritage institutions, resistance, and praxis. *Canadian Journal of Communication*, 31(3), 639–658.

Avery, L. (2015, Winter). Nobody said public engagement is easy. *Roundup*, 261, 18–21.

Barr, J. (in press). Adult education and radical museology. The role of the museum as an archive of the commons. In D. E. Clover, K. Sanford, K. Johnson, & L. Bell (Eds.), *Museums and adult education: Animating social and cultural change*. Rotterdam, The Netherlands: Sense.

Bennett, T. (1995). *The birth of the museum: History, theory, politics.* London, UK, and New York, NY: Routledge.

Boal, A. (2006). *The aesthetics of the oppressed.* London, UK: Routledge.

Borg, C., & Mayo, P. (2010, Fall). Museums: Adult education as cultural politics. *New Directions for Adult and Continuing Education*, 127, 35–43.

Butler, S., & Lehrer, E. (Eds.). (2016). *Curatorial dreams, critics imagine exhibitions.* Montreal, Canada: McGill-Queens University Press.

California Association of Museums. (2012). *Museums as third place.* Foresight Research Report. Santa Cruz, CA: Author.

Casey, D. (2007). Museums as agents for social and political change. In S. Watson (Ed.), *Museums and their communities* (pp. 292–299). London, UK: Routledge.

Chobot, M. C., & Chobot, R. B. (1990). Museums as educational institutions. *New directions for adult and continuing education, 1990*, 55 62. doi:10.1002/ace.36719904709

Clover, D. E. (2015). Adult education for social and environmental change in contemporary public art galleries and museums in Canada, Scotland and England. *International Journal of Lifelong Education, 34*(3), 300–315. doi:10.1080/02601370.2014.99

Clover, D. E., Hall, B. L., & Follen, S. (2013). *The nature of transformation: Environmental adult education* (2nd ed.). Toronto, Canada: Ontario Institute for Studies in Education.

Clover, D. E., & Stone, E. (in press). Casting light and shadow: Reflections on nonformal adult education at Tate Modern. In D. E. Clover, K. Sanford, K. Johnson, & L. Bell (Eds.), *Museums and adult education: Animating social and cultural change*. Rotterdam, The Netherlands: Sense.

Ellis, L. (2002). The backlash to access. *Engage, 11*, 40–42.

Fitchett, P., Merriweather, L., & Coffey, H. (2015). It's not a pretty picture: How teachers make meaning through lynching imagery of America's racialized past. *The History Teacher, 48*(2), 245–269.

Frost, S. (2013). Museums and sexuality. *Museum International, 65*(1–4), 16–25. doi:10.1111/muse.12029

Gray, C. (in press). St. Mungo Museum of Religious Life and Art: A space to speak, discuss and be heard. In D. E. Clover, K. Sanford, K. Johnson, & L. Bell (Eds.), *Museums and adult education: Animating social and cultural change*. Rotterdam, The Netherlands: Sense.

Gruenewald, D. A. (2008). The best of both worlds: A critical pedagogy of place. *Environmental Education Research, 14*(3), 308.

Hooper-Greenhill, E. (1992). *Museums and the shaping of knowledge*. London, UK: Routledge.

Hunter, J. (2013, March 7). NDP questions premier's mandate in backing Kitimat refinery proposal. *The Globe and Mail*. Retrieved from: http://www.theglobeandmail.com/news/british-columbia/ndp-questions-bc-premiers-mandate-in-backing-kitimat-refinery-proposal/article9489041/

Janes, R. (2008). Museums in a troubled world: Making the case for socially responsible museums. *MUSE, 26*(5), 20–25.

Kitimat, District of. (2016). *Major projects*. Retrieved from http://www.kitimat.ca/EN/main/business/invest-in-kitimat/major-projects.html

Kitimat Museum & Archives. (2016). *Energy*. Retrieved from http://www.kitimatmuseum.ca /node/24

Klein, N. (2014). *This changes everything: Capitalism vs the climate*. Toronto, Canada: Knopf.

MacDonald, G. F., & Alsford, S. (1995). Canadian museums and the representation of culture in a multicultural nation. *Cultural Dynamics, 7*(1), 15–36.

Mayo, P. (2013). Museums as sites of critical pedagogical practice. *Review of Education, Pedagogy, and Cultural Studies, 35*(2), 144–153.

McTavish, L. (2003). The decline of the modernist museum. *Acadiensis, 33*(1), 97–107.

Morton, B. (2015, November 12). Trudeau bans oil tankers on B.C.'s north coast, threatening pipeline plan. *The Vancouver Sun*. Retrieved from http://www.vancouversun.com/business/trudeau+bans+tankers+north+coast+threatening+pipeline+plan/11515875/story.html

Newman, M. (2006). *Teaching defiance*. San Francisco, CA: Jossey-Bass.

Onciul, B. (2015). *Museums, heritage and Indigenous voice: Decolonizing engagement*. New York, NY: Routledge.

Phillips, R. B. (2011). *Museum pieces: Toward the Indigenization of Canadian museums* (Vol. 7). Montreal, Canada: McGill-Queen's Press-MQUP.

Reinsborough, P. (2010). Giant whispers: Narrative power, radical imagination and a future worth fighting for. *Affinities: A Journal of Radical Theory, Culture and Action, 4*(2), 67–78.

Sandell R., & Nightingale, E. (Eds.). (2012). *Museums, equality and social justice*. London, UK, and New York, NY: Routledge.

Scott, S. (1998). Philosophies in action. In S. Scott, B. Spencer, & A. Thomas (Eds.), *Learning for life-Canadian readings in adult education* (pp. 98–106). Toronto, Canada: Thompson.

Steedman, M. (2012). *Gallery as community: Art, education, politics.* London, UK: Whitechapel Gallery.

Sumner, J. (2012). Dining on the social economy: Local, sustainable food systems and policy development. *Canadian Review of Social Policy,* (67), 30.

Szekeres, V. (2012). Representing diversity and challenging racism: The migration museum. In R. Sandell & E. Nightingale (Eds.), *Museums, equality and social justice* (pp. 142–152). London, UK, and New York, NY: Routledge.

Taylor, E. W., McKinley-Parrish, M., & Banz, R. (2010). Adult education in cultural institutions: Libraries, museums, parks and zoos. In C. E. Kasworm, A. D. Rose, & J. M. Ross-Gordon (Eds.), *Handbook of adult and continuing education* (pp. 327–336). Los Angeles, CA: Sage.

Thompson, J. (2002). *Bread and roses.* Leicester, UK: NIACE.

UNESCO. (1999). *Cultural heritage-museums, libraries and cultural heritage: Democratizing culture, creating knowledge and building bridges.* (Report 7b from the Fifth International Conference on Adult Education-CONFINTEA V). Hamburg, Germany: UNESCO Institute for Education.

Watson, S. (Ed.). (2007). *Museums and their communities.* New York, NY: Routledge.

Welton, M. (1995). *In defense of the lifeworld: Critical perspectives on adult education.* Albany: State University of New York Press.

Whyte, M. (2015, December 29). MOCCA's master plan: A modern museum for a global city. *The Star.com.* Retrieved from http://www.thestar.com/entertainment/visualarts/2015/12/29/moccas-master-plan-a-modern-museum-for-a-global-city.html

LORRAINE BELL is a PhD candidate in the Department of Leadership Studies at the University of Victoria. Correspondence: University of Victoria, Canada. lmg@uvic.ca

DARLENE E. CLOVER is a professor of adult education in leadership studies at the University of Victoria. Correspondence: University of Victoria, Canada. clover@uvic.ca

New Directions for Adult and Continuing Education • DOI: 10.1002/ace

3

This chapter focuses on the role of religiously based spirituality in cultivating environmental awareness and citizenship by examining an adult environmental education program offered at the Ignatius Jesuit Centre, a religious retreat center in Guelph, Canada.

The St. Ignatius Jesuit Retreat and Training Centre: Cultivating Ecological Awareness and Connection with the Earth

Janet Groen

You tuck the scraps we have refused to eat into the folds of Earth's apron;
And when she is due, our Mother will push and push forth new food,
Rejoicing our hearts and restoring our bodies; potatoes and tomatoes, radishes
and cabbages, strawberries and blueberries.
You repair abandoned city lots by sending your angels, the dandelions,
Who plunge their medicines deep into damaged soil suffocating
Beneath concrete slabs, tossed away bricks and gross negligence.
—Guelph Psalm excerpt, Ignatian retreatant, 2015

The 8-day silent ecospirituality retreat is coming to a close. On the last full day of our time together, we were each asked to seek out some sign of resurrection in nature—"such as the gravel pit or a compost pile ... if you are at a compost heap, imagine the food and garden bits decaying, breaking down into more 'basic' matter; imagine them slowly merging and forming into rich, wonderful humus" (*Leaning into Hope* retreat handout, 2015). Above is an excerpt from one retreatant's written response on his experience of resurrection as he sat in contemplative silence, listening to what nature had to tell him.

During the last week of July 2015, I, alongside 15 other retreatants, participated in an eco-spiritual silent retreat entitled *Leaning into Hope* at the Ignatius Jesuit Centre in Guelph, Canada. The description of this retreat follows:

We lean into hope these eight days: finding mutual sustenance, strength, light, dance of hope with God, one another and creation. Through presentations, guided walks, contemplative reflections, personal prayer, Eucharist and other

NEW DIRECTIONS FOR ADULT AND CONTINUING EDUCATION, no. 153, Spring 2017 © 2017 Wiley Periodicals, Inc.
Published online in Wiley Online Library (wileyonlinelibrary.com) • DOI: 10.1002/ace.20219

communal prayer on the land, we will explore how we might recognize and become expressions of hope alive in these difficult but grace-filled times. (The Ignatius Jesuit Centre, n.d.)

As the Ignatian exercises unfolded for the duration of this retreat, we were asked to delve into our personal stories, accept the reality of the ecological crisis and our participation in the crisis, approach creation as a contemplative experience, celebrate our storied relationship with creation and be with creation in her suffering, and, finally, to move toward a hopeful response as we prepared to leave this retreat.

This chapter focuses on the Ignatius Jesuit Centre, a religious retreat center in Guelph, Canada, and their quest to increase environmental citizenship in the broader community. I begin by providing an overview of the role religion and spirituality could play in shifting our relationship with the natural world; away from an anthropocentric individualistic stance (Taylor, 1991) toward the realization that we are deeply interconnected with each other and the natural world (Clover, 2003; Sumner, 2003). I then narrow my focus to Ignatius Jesuit Centre and how they have taken up a particular set of contemplative exercises, the Ignatian Spiritual Exercises, as a vehicle for environmental awareness and collective environmental action and citizenship.

A Spiritual Approach to Environmental Adult Education

Although there are numerous protest movements and actions aspiring to raise critical awareness of our ecological crisis and to launch environmental activism, I believe that something fundamental is missing here. The substantial change needed to address how we live in this world requires a deeper process of learning that compels us to recall our interconnection with her. We need to learn approaches that enable us to grapple with existential questions. Why we are here? What does it means to be human? Coates (2003) asked, what is our proper relationship with the world? In essence, we are called to draw on a spiritual approach of learning, "stressing the intrinsic biophysical and spiritual connection of human beings to nature" (Walter, 2009, p. 3). Indeed when many fields of study, including religion, have devised their deepest and best solutions to our crisis, the concluding statement offered at the end of their studies is, "It is really a spiritual problem—a problem of changing hearts and minds so that people will live differently" (McFague, 2013, p. 2).

Turning to a brief description of religion and spirituality, religion is based on both individual and collective relationships, belief systems and practices, while spirituality usually focuses on the individual and the quest for meaning and purpose, connection to a higher being, and being interconnected with others and the natural world (Groen, Coholic, & Graham, 2012). However, I agree with English (2012) who argued that religion and spirituality are not totally separate; "rather some people express their spirituality through religious practice (i.e., in more formalized and institutional ways) and

New Directions for Adult and Continuing Education • DOI: 10.1002/ace

others through alternative means" (English, 2012, p. 18). In addition, it is important to acknowledge the role that religious groups and, more specifically, faith-based adult educators have played in taking on issues of social justice and change (O'Sullivan, 1999) as evidenced through various initiatives such as Mondragon, the Antigonish Movement, the Highlander Center, and Frontier College (English, 2012). Finally, utilizing Hungerford and Volk's (1990) model that outlined three phases in environmental education that were involved in cultivating environmental citizenship in environmental education programming, Hitzhusen (2006, 2012) made a compelling case for the inclusion of religion and spiritual approaches to learning as we move through these phases. Specifically, Hungerford and Volk's phases go from developing initial awareness or sensitivity, to a basic understanding of the environment, on to developing the motivation to acquire skills to solve environmental problems and finally the desire to actively engage in working toward solutions to the environmental crisis at an individual and possibly a societal level. In turn, Hitzhusen (2006, 2012) suggested that undergirding these with a religiously and spiritually based sense of a moral imperative, calling, sacred awe, and a position of love for the planet and for each other can be powerful and deep motivators for both personal change and contributions to societal change.

The Ignatius Jesuit Centre

The Ignatius Jesuit Centre is a place of peace that welcomes a global community of people who seek to integrate their inner and outer life with God and with all Creation.

> We promote right relationships with God, with each other and with Creation, especially through spiritual development in the traditional of the Spiritual Exercises of St. Ignatius of Loyola and through deep engagement with this land. (Ignatius Jesuit Centre, Mission-Vision, n.d.)

This 600-acre retreat center is located on the edge of the City of Guelph in Southern Ontario. Its origins go back to 1913 when Jesuits arrived to create a training center for young men who wished to become Jesuits. While there was just a farmhouse on the property when they arrived, more housing and classrooms were built to accommodate the increasing demand for the training of Jesuits. Since the later part of the 20th century, the center has contracted substantially in size and altered its farming practices. Specifically, the college building that was devoted to training Jesuits closed and the building is now leased to businesses that share the values of the Centre, such as Wildlife Preservation Canada, The Ontario Beekeeping Association, and an Outdoor Early Childhood Program. What remains is Loyola House, in operation since 1964, a center that offers retreats based on Ignatian Spirituality (elaborated on later) and training programs for spiritual directors. The Ignatius Farm also has become a model for organic agriculture. Members of residents mentor organic gardeners through several initiatives: renting garden plots so those in the nearby city of Guelph can grow organic produce; growing and distributing organic produce through a Community Shared Agriculture Program; and offering an internship program for those interested in organic gardening. As well, an ecological restoration initiative is devoted to restoring 100 acres of its land to an old growth forest, so that we may be reminded of what existed prior to the arrival of European settlers. Finally, walking paths have been created that meander through the property, with chairs and benches placed in such a way as to invite retreatants to linger.

The Greening of Ignatian Spiritual Exercises

Retreats at Loyola House are based on the Ignatian Spiritual exercises, which were developed by Ignatius Loyola and the Society of Jesus, otherwise known as the Jesuits. St. Ignatius, whose common name is Inigo Lopez, was born in 1491 in Loyola, in the Basque region of Spain. He spent his early years in the military; however, that came to an abrupt ending when a cannonball shattered his leg and broke his right knee. During his convalescence at his childhood home, he spent time reading books about Jesus Christ and the Saints and he experienced a conversion that took him to the Abbey of Montserrat. His quest to have a deeper relationship with God led him to a life of poverty where he first helped the sick in the hospitals of Mansera, followed by time spent in isolation in a cave communing with God and the Holy Spirit. Based on his ongoing journaling of this spiritual experience, he began to direct others on how to deepen their companionship with God. Gradually, he compiled the prayers, meditation exercises, and directions into a carefully mapped framework for undertaking a retreat, calling these the *Spiritual Exercises*. As Ignatius wanted individuals to undertake these exercises in companionship, he directed his writings to experienced spiritual directors. Indeed the *Spiritual Exercises* are still to be used as "a guide for a director, mentor, or soul-friend in helping another person through prayer and reflection, discover God's action in his or her life" (Silf, 1999, pp. 16–17). His attempts to share the *Spiritual Exercises* were, rejected by the Church, who challenged his authority speak of these matters without being ordained. While studying to acquire the necessary academic qualifications in Paris in order to be ordained, he and several friends who supported each other in practicing the *Exercises*, formed the Society of Jesus and become the very first Jesuits. In 1536, he was ordained and adopted the name Ignatius.

The exercises, which are practiced in much the same way they were half a millennium ago, involve four phases that, for many people on a 30-day silent retreat, are broken down into four "weeks." Briefly, the first phase is a "time of reflection on our lives in light of God's boundless love for us" (The spiritual exercises, n.d.). Time is spent reflecting on one's life, seeing where God has been part of our life and where we have rejected God. During the second phase, the story of Christ on earth and his teachings is revisited in a quest to become closer to Christ. The third phase dwells in the suffering of Christ, culminating in his death. Finally, the fourth phase focuses on the resurrection story and the challenge to love Christ and serve him in concrete ways. During all phases, retreatants spend time in contemplation and meditation, with specific exercises given to them in a daily meeting with a spiritual director.

Almost 20 years ago, John English, a Jesuit, and two members of the newly formed Ecology Project at the Centre, built on these contemplative exercises to emphasize our connection to nature and the underlying reasons for our ecological crisis; in other words, they were greening the exercises. The development of these exercises signaled a larger shift that was going on at the centre, based on a deepening conviction that they needed to respond to the harm we were inflicting on the natural world. The Ecology Project was created and spearheaded by Jim Profit (2004), a former director of the Ignatius Centre who died in 2014, and it has now morphed into a focus on eco-spirituality. This occurs through programming, the development of the old growth forest and the organic gardens, as well as community garden shareholders and mindful development of pathways and sites that allow for individual contemplation. Currently, Yvonne Prowse, one of several of the Centre's spiritual directors, is responsible for the ecospirituality retreat programs. She, alongside Bill Clarke, a Jesuit living on-site, and Tarcia Gerwing led the program I attended. In this next section, I offer three vignettes of my experiences of participating in the greening of the Spiritual Exercises. Each vignette highlights an aspect of the Greening Exercises and link to Hitzhusen's (2006) interpretation of Hungerford and Volk's (1990) model of cultivating of environmental citizenship.

Retreatant Reflections on the Greening of the Exercises

Slow Down. According to Hungerford and Volk's (1990) model of environmental behavior, entry-level variables, which include cultivating environmental sensitivity, "are important pre-cursors to environmental behavior, and [they can] enhance a person's decision making once an action is undertaken" (Hitzhusen, 2006, p. 16). A significant aspect of environmental sensitivity calls on us to simply appreciate nature for its own intrinsic worth and to feel awe and wonder about its beauty. Hitzhusen (2006), in turn, believed that this intrinsic valuing of creation, incorporated in many religions, through the shared values of respect and reverence, can lead to a deeper love of the natural world. Turning to my experiences as a retreatant at the Ignatius Centre, an underlying strand woven through all phases of the retreat was the quest to enhance our appreciation of the Creator's handiwork that was all around us. But in order to achieve this, we needed to be nudged into paying attention, something that took me a little time. My arrival at the Ignatius Centre was on the heels of teaching a two-week doctoral seminar; followed by a week of visiting family. I could not wait to get to the Centre and move into silence. And yet, it took several days for me to slow down and be in the moment. Indeed the change in pace was initially jarring; it felt like somebody was slamming on the brakes. The rhythm of each day unfolded with a brief talk by one of the retreat facilitators, as well as an assignment to guide our experience of the day before us. The rest of time was ours, with the exception of an optional visit to an assigned spiritual director. We convened again for evening gathering. Talking was limited to the daily visit with our spiritual director and the occasional request, in our morning or evening gathering, to talk in small groups or to read something out loud that we had written.

This expansive vista of fairly unstructured time did not match the busyness of thoughts racing through my mind. During my first visit with my spiritual director, she noted my distracted mind when she zoomed in on my comment that I had lost my sunglasses on that first afternoon walk. I had absentmindedly put them on top of my baseball cap in order to take a photo. Of course, a few minutes later, when using my hat to wave off a bee, I lost my glasses. It was only much later that I noticed they were gone, forcing me to retrace my steps several times before I found them. I was not paying attention; I was not in the moment. At the close of my conversation with my spiritual director, I was given my assignment: To return the next day prepared to describe just one thing that I had noticed on one of my walks on the Ignatian property.

Paying attention and noticing what was around me was a constant thread throughout this retreat; gently suggested by my spiritual director, proffered to each of us through the various exercises designed by the facilitators, and eventually internalized by me. For example, I was able to attend to the changing light, the pause of a dragonfly, the intensity of a particular spice in the soup and the noise of the traffic on the nearby highway. In hindsight, as I consider my increased ability to pay attention to the natural world, I realize the invitational approach to experience the land helped guide this experience. The creation of sacred nooks and crannies, chairs positioned to invite rest and one's gaze over the field, and trails that meandered through a variety of landscapes created the possibility of becoming reconnected with the natural world.

Grief. The second phase of Hungerford and Volk's (1990) model asks us to take ownership for the environmental crisis by increasing our knowledge and understanding of the issues and the consequences of our behavior, both positive and negative. Hitzhusen (2006) extends this line of thinking to religions' traditions, arguing that a foundation of social justice runs through many of them; which, in turn, calls on people of faith to actively commit to some aspect of the environmental crisis as part of their overarching responsibility to work toward peace and care for all beings on this planet. In this retreat, the first few days were devoted to teaching us about the natural story not only of this particular setting as it shifted from being an old growth forest, to farmland and orchards, but also of the stations of the cosmos; a visual representation of the unfolding story of the universe. And then we were called into a place of grief and loss, where we were asked to acknowledge the profound impact of our actions on the natural world, locally and beyond. The third morning, as we walked into the chapel, we sat around a wheelbarrow of topsoil. As we contemplated this soil, we were reminded that it was becoming increasingly sterile as it was separated from its nutrient rich environment. The links between the sterility of the soil and sterility of our nature were quickly and powerfully made when Yvonne spoke of the soil in drought beleaguered California. From there her reflection unspooled to other examples of how we have abused our environment, turning away from a loving and caring relationship with our world, to one that caused it deep harm and pain. As Yvonne's talk came to a close, we were asked to take the day to reflect on the losses the natural world has experienced and to bring our sorrows to our evening gathering, which would take place in the Jesuit cemetery. While this is a painful experience, ecologists Macy and Johnstone (2012) affirm the necessity of this grief, telling us we need to move through this pain into active engagement and hope.

Connection to Our Future. In the final phase of Hungerford and Volk's (1990) model, we begin to feel that we can play an important role in resolving environmental issues; we are empowered. Hitzhusen (2006) believes that these qualities of motivation and empowerment are deeply reinforced in religious traditions and that hopeful engagement in creating a vision that may not be realized in our lifetime is what faith is all about. "Such a vision may provide a source of enduring hope for those facing environmental challenges of the present—this generation may not see all its hopes come to pass, but present efforts can still help the next generation inherit a better world" (p. 18).

Returning to the example offered at the outset of this article, we were asked to lean into hopeful engagement by seeking out signs of resurrection or new growth in nature on the grounds of the Centre, and to notice ways that we feel compelled to engage in the work of "healing the world and giving hope … I continue to notice any particular concerns for the world that arise in me, in love, and whether there is some specific action for the healing of our world that I feel drawn to" (Prowse, 2015. Leaning into hope [Retreat handout]). After a day of silent and thoughtful contemplation, we came together to share our readings, our poetry and our stories of hopeful reengagement. The energy of committing to hardworking hope on behalf of the natural world within the space was palpable.

Now that I reflect on this retreat a few months later, the obvious question remains as to whether the energy and motivation I experienced has been sustained. At a personal level, some small things have certainly changed; in particular, the caution offered to me by my spiritual director to "pay attention" has stayed with me. The beauty of nature is all around us if we simply notice. Shifting my gaze to my teaching practice, I have begun to explore ways to incorporate the emotion of "grief" in my classroom work on environmental education. While I am in the preliminary stages of this journey, considering the role of arts-based activities to support adult learners through this process,

I have come to realize that in order to work toward hopeful engagement in ecojustice, we must first acknowledge what we have lost.

Concluding Thoughts

In May 2015, Pope Francis released an encyclical letter entitled *On Care for Our Common Home*, signaling a profound demonstration of the central role religion and spirituality should play in addressing our environmental crisis. In this encyclical letter, Pope Francis (2015) outlined the ecological crisis, drew from religious traditions to increase our commitment to the environment, explored the roots of our current malaise, and finally offered suggestions and dialogue for engagement, including guidelines for international policy direction and environmental approaches. The spotlight Pope Francis has placed on the roles and responsibilities of religious and spiritual traditions should play in addressing the degradation of the planet are reflected in shift that the St. Ignatius Centre has undertaken in placing care and love of the natural world at the heart of their mandate. Indeed, over the past decade, beyond the implicit beauty of the grounds and the ethic of responsibility enacted in their farming practices, the staff have developed overt environmental adult education programs and have led the way for other retreat centers to follow in their footsteps. These programs, based on the greening of the Ignatian Spiritual Exercises, mindfully encourage retreatants to grow from a place of awe and intrinsic appreciation of nature, toward recognition and ownership of the environmental crisis and finally into a place of response or action. Their work in this area serves as a powerful example how the intertwining of religion and spirituality within environmental adult education programming can move us from complacency toward the courage required to enact a way of living that demonstrates that we are all deeply connected with each other and the world around us.

References

Clover, D. E. (2003). Environmental adult education: Critique and creativity in a globalizing world. In D. Clover & L. Hill (Eds.), *New directions for adult and continuing education: No. 99. Environmental adult education: Ecological learning, theory, and practice for socioenvironmental change* (pp. 5–15). New York, NY: Wiley.

Coates, J. (2003). *Ecology and social work: Toward a new paradigm*. Halifax, Canada: Fernwood Press.

English, L. (2012). For whole purposes? Examining the spirituality agenda in adult education. In J. Groen, D. Coholic, & J. Graham (Eds.), *Spirituality in education and social work: Theory, practice and pedagogies* (pp. 17–33). Waterloo, Canada: Wilfrid Laurier Press.

Francis. (2015). *Encyclical letter: Laudato si on care for our common home*. Retrieved from http://w2.vatican.va/content/francesco/en/encyclicals/documents/papa-francesco_20150524_enciclica-laudato-si.html

Groen, J., Coholic, D., & Graham, J. (Eds.). (2012). *Spirituality in education and social work: Theory, practice and pedagogies*. Waterloo, Canada: Wilfrid Laurier Press.

Hitzhusen, G. E. (2006). Religion and environmental education: Building on common ground. *Canadian Journal of Environmental Education, 11*, 9–25.

Hitzhusen, G. E. (2012). Going green and renewing life: Environmental education in faith communities. In E. P. Isaac (Ed.), *New directions for adult and continuing education: No. 133. Expanding the boundaries of adult religious education: Strategies, techniques, and partnerships for the new millennium* (pp. 35–44). San Francisco, CA: Jossey-Bass.

Hungerford, H.R., & Volk, T. L. (1990). Changing learner behavior through environmental education. *Journal of Environmental Education, 21*(3), 8–21.

Ignatian Retreatant. (2015). *Guelph psalm.* Guelph, ON: Ignatius Jesuit Centre.

Ignatius Jesuit Centre. (n.d.). *Vision and mission.* Retrieved from http://ignatiusguelph.ca/about/mission-vision/

Ignatius Jesuit Centre. (n.d.). *Loyola House: Retreat & Training Centre. Programs 2015–2016.* Guelph, ON: Author.

Macy, J., & Johnstone, C. (2012). *Active hope: How to face this mess we're in without going crazy.* Novato, CA: New World Library.

McFague, S. (2013). *Blessed are the consumers: Climate change and the practice of restraint.* Minneapolis, MN: Fortress Press.

O'Sullivan, E. (1999). *Transformative learning: Educational vision for the 21st century.* New York, NY: Zed Books, in association with the University Toronto Press.

Profit, J. (2004). Spiritual exercises and ecology. *Promotio Justitiae, 82,* 6–11.

Prowse, Y. (2015). *Learning into hope* [Retreat handout]. Guelph, ON: Ignatius Jesuit Centre.

Silf, M. (1999). *Inner compass: An invitation to Ignatian spirituality.* Chicago, IL: Loyola Press.

The Spiritual Exercises. (n.d.). *In Ignatian spirituality.* Retrieved from http://www.ignatianspirituality.com/ignatian-prayer/the-spiritual-exercises

Sumner, J. (2003). Environmental adult education and community sustainability. In D. Clover & L. Hill (Eds.), *New directions for adult and continuing education: No. 99. Environmental adult education: Ecological learning, theory, and practice for socioenvironmental change* (pp. 39–45). New York, NY: Wiley.

Taylor, C. (1991). *The malaise of modernity.* Toronto, Canada: House of Anansi Press.

Walter, P. (2009). Philosophies of adult environmental education. *Adult Education Quarterly, 60*(1), 3–25.

JANET GROEN is an associate professor in adult learning, Werklund School of Education, University of Calgary, Calgary, Canada.

4

This chapter describes the role small-scale organic farmers are playing as adult educators in alternative food networks and as leaders for food systems transformation. Findings are drawn from a survey of organic farmers in British Columbia, Western Canada.

Adult Learning in Alternative Food Networks

Catherine Etmanski, Ingrid Kajzer Mitchell

On September 18, 2013, the United Nations Conference on Trade and Development (UNCTAD) released a 340-page report on the topic of sustainable agriculture and its links to food security in the current era of climate change. The report indicated that a fundamental paradigm shift is needed in agricultural development. Contributing authors suggested that we must move from conventional industrial agriculture toward more sustainable practices. Moreover, the report recognized that "a farmer is not only a producer of agricultural goods, but also a manager of an agro-ecological system" (UNCTAD, p. i).

The pages that follow expand on this idea that a farmer is more than simply a food producer. In recent publications, Etmanski (e.g., 2012, 2015) has argued that small-scale organic farmers are key leaders in food systems transformation and educators addressing the complex socio-economic and environmental challenges we face today. This chapter builds on earlier work to present preliminary survey findings from a case study located on Vancouver Island and the surrounding Gulf Islands. The chapter is organized as follows: We begin by situating the organic farming movement as a "food justice" response to the detrimental impacts of global industrial agriculture. We then describe the intersection of food and adult learning, laying the ground for farmers' descriptions of informal, incidental, and self-directed learning, as well as their experiences of action learning on their farms. We expand on this by describing how strong alternative food networks (AFNs), such as the organic farming movement, provide fertile ground for learning. This context is followed by an introduction of the case study and then an overview and discussion of our preliminary findings. We conclude by raising areas of caution and articulating the next steps in this study.

New Directions for Adult and Continuing Education, no. 153, Spring 2017 © 2017 Wiley Periodicals, Inc.
Published online in Wiley Online Library (wileyonlinelibrary.com) • DOI: 10.1002/ace.20220

Organic Farming as a "Food Justice" Response to Industrial Agriculture

Various movements associated with food have emerged in response to the current state of global industrial agriculture. As Etmanski (2012, 2015) has documented, the list of social, economic, and environmental problems—indeed crises—associated with the dominant agricultural paradigm is extensive. This list includes depletion of soils, as well as groundwater pollution leading to oceanic dead zones; unethical treatment of both people and animals; food waste and dumping of subsidized grains in the Global South; contamination of genetically modified (GM) seeds into non-GM crops; and the multiple ways in which industrial agriculture contributes to greenhouse gases causing climate change, including through the overuse of natural gas and oil.

Many challenges stem from the technological and chemical changes to agriculture during the so-called Green Revolution, which ultimately "proved to be unsustainable as it damaged the environment, caused dramatic loss of biodiversity and associated traditional knowledge, [favored] wealthier farmers, and left many poor farmers deeper in debt" (Altieri, 2009, p. 102). Kesavan and Malarvannan (2010) suggested that "today, it is widely acknowledged that the 'yield gains' associated with the green revolution of the 1960s and 1970s have tapered off largely because of deterioration in the structure, quality and fertility of the soil" (p. 908). In addition, the use of certain pesticides in treating seeds has been linked to the worldwide decline of the honeybee population (Krupke, Hunt, Eitzer, Andino, & Given, 2012), and scientists have been calling for further investigation into links between the general use of pesticides or herbicides and the occurrence of cancer in both children (Hoar Zahm & Ward, 1998) and adults (Dich, Hoar Zahm, Hanberg, & Adami, 1997). Moreover, the increase in fast-food outlets has caused some urban inner cities to become known as food deserts, that is, impoverished neighborhoods, which are "a long car ride from the nearest supermarkets and sources of healthy food" (Walter, 2012). The list of food-related ecological injustices goes on.

People in many parts of the world have been taking action at both the local and global level to resist and transform the dominant industrial agricultural system through calls for food security, food sovereignty, and food justice (Alkon & Agyeman, 2011). Using a concept derived from environmental and/or ecological approaches to justice (as described elsewhere in this volume), proponents of "food justice" critically analyze and denounce the ways in which industrial agriculture disproportionately disadvantages women, people of color, and people living in poverty, while promoting grassroots efforts to transition to a more equitable agricultural system (Holt-Giménez, 2011, p. 323). Although the terms food security, food sovereignty, and food justice express various degrees of social critique and politicization (Holt-Giménez, 2011), for the purpose of this chapter, suffice it to say that the organic farmers who became participants in this study are all working toward food justice, to greater or lesser degrees, in the context of localized food production on their own farms. A desire to transform the dominant food system, that is, fundamentally shift the current state of global industrial agriculture, underlies much this work for food justice.

Having introduced the context of organic farming, we now explore the intersection of adult learning and food.

Strong Alternative Food Networks (AFNs) as Sites of Adult Learning

Adult educators have long been concerned with action-oriented learning in the workplace (Lewin, 1997; Zuber-Skerritt, 2002). However, the explicit exploration of workplace learning on the farm, that is, the scholarly intersection of food and adult learning is relatively recent. In Canada, the 2006 annual Canadian Association for the Study of Adult Education (CASAE) conference is cited as one of the first explorations of food and adult education (Sumner, 2013). Since that 2006 roundtable discussion, food as a topic of investigation has gradually been gaining momentum in adult education communities in different parts of the world, yielding new publications, conference presentations, graduate level courses, and research projects (e.g., Sumner, 2015; Swan & Flowers, 2015).

Of particular interest to this study are the ways in which food is intersecting with topics already familiar to adult educators, such as: self-directed and informal approaches to learning (Everson, 2015; Smith, 2015). Regarding informal learning in social action, Foley (1999) suggested, "The most interesting and significant learning occurs informally and incidentally, in people's everyday lives" (p. 1). This sentiment is echoed by pioneer food scholar Jennifer Sumner (2013), who aptly observed, "Food-related learning is happening all around us, whether adult educators recognize it or not" (p. 195). Just as the editors of this sourcebook argue that more widespread ecological changes warrant adult educators' attention, given the challenges perpetrated by the dominant food system outlined earlier, we (the authors and researchers) believe that it is timely to attend to the de facto role of farmers who are already playing as educators.

Goodman and Goodman (2007) defined Alternative Food Networks (AFNs) as

> New and rapidly mainstreaming spaces in the food economy defined by— among other things—the explosion of organic, Fair Trade, and local, quality, and premium specialty foods [... in which] the production and consumption of food are more closely tied together spatially, economically, and socially. (p. 208)

Follett (2009) argued that the organic farming movement can be divided into two movements: corporate or "weak" AFNs and "strong" AFNs. The weak corporate version embodying large-scale industrial organic food production does focus on protecting the environment, but tends to neglect issues concerning food justice, that is, equity and social justice for rural communities, small-scale farm owners, or laborers in the agricultural system. The strong, local, and smaller version of organic AFNs not only embrace environmental protection, "but they also address the issues that weak alternatives neglect" (Follett, 2009, p. 31) such as production scale, farm size, and promoting alternative market relationships.

By way of example, strong AFNs reveal more of a direct relationship between farmers and consumers, and, unlike weak corporate versions, their networks focus more directly on relationship, transparency, and trust (Follet, 2009). As strong AFNs, it can be argued that small-scale organic farmers are potentially better positioned to create social and political change (Follett, 2009), particularly due to the indirect impacts of learning (Forssell & Lankoski, 2015).

In this study, we are curious about the potential for learning in strong AFNs where relationship, transparency, and trust are present. An emerging body of empirical work suggests there is evidence of learning taking place in alternative food networks (Kajzer Mitchell, Low, Davenport, & Brigham, forthcoming; Seyfang, 2006). As is described in the next section, there is likewise evidence to suggest that farmers surveyed in this study are cultivating relationships of trust with their customers through direct sales from their farms and interactions during markets. These conversations and relationships, we believe, create fertile soil for adult learning in general and action, informal, and self-directed learning in particular.

The Case Study

Vancouver Island and the surrounding Gulf Islands are located on the southern coast of British Columbia, Canada. In the period of 2012–2014, British Columbia experienced the largest growth in organic producers in Canada (Canada Organic Trade Association [COABC], 2016). The province is demonstrating promising leadership with regard to organic food and farming and is actively seeking to grow the organic sector (COABC, 2015). Within this context, Vancouver Island is emerging as a "foodie destination" (Canadian Broadcasting Corporation [CBC], 2015), and as particularly fertile ground for the development and promotion of alternative food movements such as the organic food movement. At the time this study was conducted, the Certified Organic Associations of BC (COABC) search page (COABC, n.d.) listed 87 certified organic farms on Vancouver Island and the surrounding Gulf Islands.

In early spring of 2016, we (Ingrid and Catherine) had the opportunity to survey 31 small-scale organic farmers in this region. The survey is part of a larger study examining ways in which farmers are demonstrating learning, teaching, and leadership within the small-scale organic agriculture movement.

New Directions for Adult and Continuing Education • DOI: 10.1002/ace

The objective of the survey was to gain some preliminary data that would help us better understand whether small-scale organic farmers in our region are perceiving themselves as educators of more sustainable practices and leaders in food system transformation and how they are enacting this education and leadership in their networks.

More specifically, the approximately 20-minute survey included 30 questions, which served to develop a demographic profile of the sample and elicit motivations behind organic farming, attitudes toward learning and food system transformation, and the specific nature of any educational initiatives. The survey was sent to the 87 small-scale organic farms, compiled from farms listed on the COABC website in April 2016. The survey elicited a response rate of 36% (31 respondents). It is important to note that we differentiated between farms and organic food processors and our findings focus solely on farm operations.

The majority of farmers participating in the study average less than $50,000 (many less than $25,000) in yearly income and thus can be described as small in scale. The majority of farmers surveyed own their own land, with 71% of the farmers having 10 or more years of experience farming in general, and 26% operating with less than 4 years. More than half of the respondents (58%) have 10-plus years of experience farming *organically*, 19% had 5–9 years, and finally, 23% had 1–4 years of experience of organic farming. How respondents came to farming differed greatly: for some, it was a career, life transition, or lifestyle decision (e.g., wanting to lead a healthier life and grow their own food). For others, it was because of previous experience with farming and coming from a farming family background.

Some of the goods produced by the surveyed farmers include: livestock/poultry, flowers, herbs, mushrooms, and seeds; however, vegetables, fruit, and berries were listed as the most common. Although wholesale and retail sales are important distribution channels, a total of 94% of farmers sell directly to consumers, for example, at farmers' markets, stores on a farm, farm stands, and via organic food box programs. Moreover, the farmers surveyed also sell directly to local restaurants, caterers, and chefs. The relationships strengthened through these direct sales support previously mentioned scholarly research on strong AFNs.

Perceptions and Attitudes of Small-Scale Organic Farmers

The premise of this chapter is that farmers are more than producers, and organic food is more than just an object of market exchange. In order to better understand how adult education is demonstrated within the small-scale organic agricultural movement, we need to better understand farmers' own lived experiences, that is, their perceptions and attitudes. With 74% stating they do actively educate consumers and other members of their network about organic farming, it becomes apparent there is a strong educational component to small-scale organic farming. The perception of

New Directions for Adult and Continuing Education • DOI: 10.1002/ace

their changing role from producers alone to educators and leaders in food system transformation may be revealed by their perception of farmers' roles more broadly speaking, as well as their perceived individual roles and impact (Table 4.1).

Farmers surveyed unanimously "strongly agreed" or "agreed" that farmers in general have a role to play in food system transformation. Furthermore, more than 70% regarded themselves as personally having an active role in this transformation. It becomes apparent, however, that some farmers surveyed also felt neutral or even disagreed with this statement. As we look closer at the data and examine the extent to which farmers feel they have a role to play in *teaching* about food system transformation, we also begin to see that many farmers clearly perceive themselves as farmers first and foremost, and the educator role is secondary. Also, close to a majority of respondents felt it beneficial for consumers to have a close relationship with farmers. Thirty-nine percent of farmers felt neutral about the extent to which they individually are making a significant educational difference in teaching people about organic farming.

In order to explore how small-scale organic farmers enact and express their individual and collective roles as educators, the respondents in the survey were asked questions related to *whom* they educate and *what* they educate *about*. In response to our open-ended questions "who do you educate?"; that is, who is the "student" or "learner," respondents shared with us a far reaching list including friends and family, other farmers, customers, student groups and teachers, farm colleagues/employees and volunteers, customers (e.g., consumers, restaurant workers/owner/chefs) and also the general public and community members at large. Other audiences included members of local food initiatives (e.g., the Comox Valley Seed Savers) and even conference attendees and local government. Some farmers identified more with their role as educators stating, "The classroom is wherever I am and includes me as the student and the educator." In response to the survey question "what do you educate people about?" the most frequently stated areas were organic growing practices (81%), organic farming standards (65%), and their own lived experience as a farmer (81%). Other areas included health and food quality, food security, land use, ecological systems, and organic food preparation (e.g., recipes, storage, preservation/freezing of foods). Educating others about small-scale organic farming business practices, economics of food systems, and food marketing were also highlighted.

It is evident that farmers are mainly engaging in informal adult education, by informally sharing and co-creating knowledge with various members of their network(s). They undertake this informal educational role through casual conversations with consumers at the farmers' markets, during farm tours, at farm stands, or via public speaking or workshop opportunities in schools, community centers or other public venues. Interestingly, while the majority of respondents perceived their own farm to be the main "classroom," in person communication at farmers' markets was by far the most common

Table 4.1. Farmers' perceptions of regarding the relationship between farming and leadership, learning and education: For each statement, please indicate the extent to which you agree or disagree

	Strongly agree	Agree	Neutral	Disagree	Strongly disagree	Do not know
A. Farmers in general have a role to play in food systems transformation	24	6				1
E. I personally have an active role in leading food systems transformation	14	8	6	1		
C. Farmers in general have a role to play in teaching about food systems transformation	13	15	2			
D. I personally play a role in teaching about food systems transformation	12	10	7	1		
E. It's beneficial for consumers to have a close relationship with farmers	24	6	1			
F. I feel that I am making a significant educational difference in teaching people about organic farming	10	6	12	2		1
C. Organic farmers in this local community are well respected	12	14	2	1	1	1

way to engage with network members. Informal learning also takes place at organic farming committee or council meetings. Half of the participants surveyed stated that they sit on councils or committees related to organic farming (e.g., Small Scale Food Processors Association, Farmer Market Associations, Vancouver Island Organic Collective, and Island Organic Producer Association). Interestingly, here many are assuming leadership roles as vice presidents, board of directors, and board members. Informal sharing of knowledge is also occurring through the creation of educational material such as how-to books on small-scale organic farming, (e.g., *All the Dirt* by Fisher, Stretch, & Tunnicliffe, 2012), factsheets, blog posts, and newsletters sharing cooking recipes and information on topics such as organic farming and food preservation.

As part of understanding how farmers educate consumers and other members of their network, it becomes important to understand how farmers themselves continue to learn about organic farming practices, techniques, and trends. Our findings reveal that there appear to be three means of learning (1) informal, (2) self-directed, and (3) action learning. Ninety-four percent of farmers surveyed indicated they learn from experimentation (action learning). Interestingly, 65% of farmers also noted personal life experiences as a source of inspiration for their work. These findings are in line with the work of Franz, Piercy, Donaldson, Richard, and Westbrook (2010) who found that farmers learn by relying mostly on firsthand experiences. Ninety percent of our survey participants included farming colleagues (informal learning) as a means of learning. Blogs/magazines (84%), websites/webinars (81%), and podcasts (self-directed learning) were also important means for continued learning. Self-directed learning clearly is important for farmers as adult educators. Seventy-one percent of farmers surveyed also selected books on organic farming and food as a major source of inspiration for their farming work (e.g., how-to books and organic farmers' business handbooks). Interestingly, close to half of the respondents also indicated that nature itself, including farm animals, inspired them in their work.

In terms of what prevents farmers from teaching more people about organic farming, it is not lack of consumer interests; rather, it is lack of time. Fifty-two percent stated time constraints due to other competing farming responsibilities as a limiting factor. In the words of one participant, "I'm really stretched to get basics done right now." Farmers with less than 5 years of experience also suggested that their own perceived lack of qualifications and experience were barriers. There were, of course, some respondents who shared that education was not something they did in addition to their day-to-day farming operations. Interestingly, the majority of those who responded "no" also indicated they were not interested in assuming the role of an "educator." Some reasons for this are lack of interest and will, perceived opportunities, lack of prerequisite knowledge, qualifications or experience, and the financial costs.

New Directions for Adult and Continuing Education • DOI: 10.1002/ace

Discussion and Next Steps: The Potential for Transformative Learning in Strong AFNs

This nonrepresentative survey offered a window into the experiences of 31 organic farmers located on Vancouver Island and the surrounding Gulf Islands. It did not, nor did it intend to yield findings that could be generalized to the global organic farming movement. However, as described earlier, findings suggested that, in addition to their primary responsibility as farmers, the majority of these individuals are actively engaged as informal educators within their networks. They learn from and with one another and teach consumers in a range of different venues. This is in line with Kajzer Mitchell et al. (forthcoming) who propose that learning in AFNs is often incidental in nature and often a by-product of other activities. In addition to this informal learning, farmers themselves actively engage in self-directed learning (through books, films, online resources, etc.) and action learning as they "learn, as they live, through their experiences, in their struggles" (Foley, 1999, p. 1) navigating the everyday challenges of their workplaces (i.e., on their farms).

We propose that the informal, self-directed, and action-based learning mentioned earlier constitute creative pedagogical processes (Swan & Flowers, 2015). As farmers are engaging with network members, whether at the farmers' markets or during farm visits and tours, they are producing, sharing, and co-creating knowledge. These kinds of interactions are key in mobilizing and informing participants' understanding of food (cf. the work of Green & Duhn, 2015); supporting the creation of more meaningful relationships with other species (e.g., farm animals); and increasing awareness of the complexity and interrelatedness of the earth's life support system (cf. Davila & Dyball, 2015).

Although our preliminary findings suggest that organic farmers are indeed playing a role in education for food systems transformation, the degree to which transformative learning may be taking place within the scope of this case study is yet to be determined. Following the work of scholars such as Kerton and Sinclair (2010) and Levkoe (2005), we intend to explore the transformative potential of engaging with organic food and farmers through follow-up farm visits and interviews with both farmers and their consumers. Meanwhile, as we prepare for the next stage of this research, we will attend to two areas of caution: sharing responsibility for education and critically reflecting on knowledge from all sources. Scholars, public servants, and citizens in general each have a role to play in both educating the public about the detrimental ecological effects of mainstream farming practices and transforming food systems to become more sustainable. As supported by the earlier findings, it is unrealistic to expect farmers to bear the burden of responsibility for education while also attending to the year-round and daily upkeep of their farms and businesses. Moreover, it is naive to allow any one person's knowledge to stand as the unquestioned truth; academics' and politicians' knowledge is subject to limitations, biases, and oversights, as is the knowledge of even the most experienced and well-read farmer. As such, mitigating what

New Directions for Adult and Continuing Education • DOI: 10.1002/ace

Langer (forthcoming) terms "maladaptive learning" and paying attention not only to whose knowledge counts (Flowers & Swan, 2011), but also to critical thinking is essential in ongoing exploration of learning in the organic food movement.

Acknowledgments

We thank the organic farmers who so willingly shared their opinions and experiences by contributing to the survey. We also acknowledge and thank our research assistant, Roberto Melfi, for his help with our primary research. Our research has been supported by two internal research grants from Royal Roads University (IGR 15-10 and IGR 15-15).

References

Alkon, A. H., & Agyeman, J. (Eds.). (2011). *Cultivating food justice: Race, class, and sustainability*. Cambridge, MA: MIT Press.

Altieri, M. A. (2009, July–August). Agroecology, small farms, and food sovereignty. *Monthly Review*, 102–113.

Canada Organic Trade Association. (2016). *Organic agriculture in Canada: By the numbers 2012–2014*. Retrieved from https://ota.com/sites/default/files/By%20The%20Numbers-%20Organic%20Agriculture%20in%20Canada%20V2.pdf

Canadian Broadcasting Company. (2015). *Vancouver Island foodie destinations you must try*. Retrieved from http://www.cbc.ca/news/canada/british-columbia/vancouver-island-foodie-destinations-you-must-try-1.3148151

Certified Organic Associations of BC. (2015). *Plans underway to grow B.C. organic sector*. Retrieved from http://www.certifiedorganic.bc.ca/infonews/newsmedia/2015AGRIMandatoryPressRelease.pdf

Certified Organic Associations of BC. (n.d.). *Search by region*. Retrieved from http://www.certifiedorganic.bc.ca/

Davila, F., & Dyball, R. (2015). Transforming food systems through food sovereignty: An Australian urban context. *Australian Journal of Environmental Education*, 31(1), 34–45. doi:10.1017/aee.2015.14

Dich, J., Hoar Zahm, S., Hanberg, A., & Adami, H-O. (1997). Pesticides and cancer. *Cancer Causes & Control*, 8(3), 420–443.

Etmanski, C. (2012). Inch by inch, row by row: Social movement learning on Three Oaks organic farm. In B. Hall, D. E. Clover, J. Crowther, & E. Scandrett (Eds.), *Learning and education for a better world: The role of social movements* (pp. 155–167). Rotterdam, the Netherlands: Sense.

Etmanski, C. (2015). Guest editorial: Introduction to adult learning and food. *Studies in the Education of Adults*, 47(2), 120–127.

Everson, C. (2015). Growing opportunities: CSA members, CSA farmers, and informal learning in the USA. *Studies in the Education of Adults*, 47(2), 176–184.

Fisher, R., Stretch, H., & Tunnicliffe, R. (2012). *All the dirt*. Victoria, BC: Touchwood.

Flowers, R., & Swan, E. (2011). "Eating at us": Representations of knowledge in the activist documentary film Food, Inc. *Studies in the Education of Adults*, 43(2), 234–250.

Foley, G. (1999). *Learning in social action: A contribution to understanding informal education*. London, UK: Zed Books.

Follett, J. (2009). Choosing a food future: Differentiating among alternative food options. *Journal of Agricultural Environmental Ethics*, 22, 31–51.

Forssell, S., & Lankoski, L. (2015). The sustainability promise of alternative food networks: An examination through "alternative" characteristics. *Agricultural Human Values, 32,* 63–75.

Franz, N., Piercy, F., Donaldson, J., Richard, R., & Westbrook, J. (2010). Farmers learn: Implications for agricultural educators. *Journal of Rural Social Sciences, 25*(1), 37–59.

Goodman, D., & Goodman, M. (2007). Alternative food networks. In R. Kitchin & N. Thrift (Eds.), *International Encyclopedia of Human Geography* (pp. 208–220). Oxford, UK: Elsevier, 2009.

Green, M., & Duhn, I. (2015). The force of gardening: investigating children's learning in a food garden. *Australian Journal of Environmental Education, 31*(1), 60–73. doi:10.1017/aee.2014.45

Hoar Zahm, S., & Ward, M. H. (1998). Pesticides and childhood cancer. *Environmental Health Perspectives, 106*(3), 893–908.

Holt-Giménez, E. (2011). Food security, food justice, or food sovereignty?: Crises, food movements, and regime change. In A. H. Alkon & J. Agyeman (Eds.), *Cultivating food justice: Race, class, and sustainability* (pp. 310–330). Cambridge: Massachusetts Institute of Technology.

Kajzer Mitchell, I., Low, W., Davenport, E., & Brigham, T. (forthcoming). Out of the wild and in to the kitchen: Learning about sustainability through wild food products. In C. Etmanski (Ed.), *Leadership and learning for global food systems transformation.* Rotterdam, the Netherlands: Sense.

Kerton, S., & Sinclair, J. (2010). Buying local organic food: A pathway to transformative learning. *Agriculture and Human Values, 27*(4), 401–413.

Kesavan, P. C., & Malarvannan, S. (2010). Green to evergreen revolution: Ecological and evolutionary perspectives in pest management. *Current Science, 99*(7), 908–914.

Krupke, C. H., Hunt, G. J., Eitzer, B. D., Andino, G., & Given, K. (2012). Multiple routes of pesticide exposure for honey bees living near agricultural fields. *PLoS ONE, 7*(1), 1–8.

Langer, C. (forthcoming). Maladaptive learning: Incorporating institutional barriers into nonprofit community garden programming. In C. Etmanski (Ed.), *Leadership and learning for global food systems transformation.* Rotterdam, the Netherlands: Sense.

Levkoe, C. Z. (2005). Learning democracy through food justice movements. *Agriculture and Human Values, 23*(1), 89–98.

Lewin, K. (1997). *Resolving social conflicts and field theory in social science.* Washington, DC: American Psychological Association. v 422 pp. doi:10.1037/10269-000

Seyfang, G. (2006). Ecological citizenship and sustainable consumption: Examining local organic food networks. *Journal of Rural Studies, 22*(4), 383–385. doi:10.1016/j.jrurstud.2006.01.003

Smith, A. (2015). The farm wife mystery school: Women's use of social media in the contemporary North American urban homestead movement. *Studies in the Education of Adults, 47*(2), 142–159.

Sumner, J. (2013). Adult education and food: Eating as praxis. In T. Nesbit, S.M. Brigham, N. Taber, & T. Gibb (Eds.), *Building on critical traditions: Adult education and learning in Canada* (pp. 194–203). Toronto, Canada: Thompson.

Sumner, J. (2015). Reading the world: Food literacy and the potential for food system transformation. *Studies in the Education of Adults, 47*(2), 127–141.

Swan, E., & Flowers, R. (2015). Clearing up the table: Food pedagogies and environmental education—contributions, challenges and future agendas. *Australian Journal of Environmental Education, 3*(1), 146–164.

United Nations Conference on Trade and Development (UNCTAD). (2013, September 18). *Wake up before it is too late: Make agriculture truly sustainable now for food security in a changing climate. Trade and development review 2013.* Retrieved from http://unctad.org/en/PublicationsLibrary/ditcted2012d3_en.pdf

Walter, P. (2012). Educational alternatives in food production, knowledge, and consumption: The public pedagogies of Growing Power and Tsyunhehkw. *Australian Journal of Adult Learning, 52*(3), 573–594.

Zuber-Skerritt, O. (2002). The concept of action learning. *Learning Organization, 9*(3), 114–124.

CATHERINE ETMANSKI *is an associate professor and the acting director of the School of Leadership Studies at Royal Roads University.*

INGRID KAJZER MITCHELL *is an associate professor in the School of Business at Royal Roads University.*

This paper describes the key principles of an ecojustice approach to adult education. The author describes the cultural roots of the ecological crisis, the difference between ecological and individual intelligence and the linguistic colonization of the present by the past. The dangers of an overreliance on print are described and the need for a revitalization of the cultural commons is included.

An Ecojustice Approach to Educational Reform in Adult Education

Chet A. Bowers

We are in a time of ecological crisis. Consumer culture, urbanization, and the adoption of Western middle-class values continue to contribute to the overuse of natural resources and climate change caused by greenhouse gases. Our lifestyles are also undermining various cultural traditions including indigenous languages and sustainable practices that have existed for thousands of years (Brown, 2008; Klein, 2014).

Moreover, the ecological cultural crisis is not currently being addressed in education because much of what is promoted in public schools and universities reflects the thinking and patterns of action that have promoted the very crises we now face. Public schools, community organizations, and universities continue to perpetuate the middle-class values of individualism, personal freedom, and unending progress that still do not take account of environmental limits (Bowers, 2011b).

Only as adult education addresses these challenges will there be the possibility of altering the course of our current environmental and cultural crisis. An ecologically informed adult education should lead to a general rethinking of the core of education and the processes inherent within it. The problem is that the current content of adult education has a heavy emphasis on individualization and career success—both of which will be challenged in the years ahead as 9.5 billion people struggle to sustain life while natural resources become more limited. Indeed, the situation is not a problem *of* education but a problem *in* education because universities and other public educational entities have been uncritically accepting of and adherent to the larger economic and political forces that undermine the environment and sustainable cultural life. We need to teach and learn differently (Orr, 2004).

New Directions for Adult and Continuing Education, no. 153, Spring 2017 © 2017 Wiley Periodicals, Inc.
Published online in Wiley Online Library (wileyonlinelibrary.com) • DOI: 10.1002/ace.20221

Principles of Ecojustice Adult Education

Professors and adult and community educators might begin by regarding educational reforms within a paradigm that does not colonize other cultures, and that provides an awareness of community-centered traditions that enable people to live less consumer and thus less environmentally destructive lives. The most promising way to do this is to focus on understanding of the ecology of all life systems—including the nature of sustainable communities. For many years, I have called this paradigm shift an ecojustice approach to educational reform (Bowers, 2006, 2011a, 2012). The following are the guiding principles (Bowers, 2012).

Eliminating Eco-Racism. Marginalized groups in poor, low-income communities of color in different parts of the world are disproportionately victimized by the effects of environmental degradation. Millions of tons of toxic chemicals produced by the industrialized systems are dumped in these community sites. The soil, water, air, plants, and animals—indeed the basis of all life-forming and sustaining processes—are being threatened in these communities. The West's tradition of equating increases in consumerism with progress impacts these marginalized social groups.

Eliminating the Colonization of Other Cultures. Colonization continues to take both the traditional forms of appropriating resources and the processes of promoting Western values and patterns of thinking. The digital revolution now promotes a pattern of thinking that undermines the face-to-face intergenerational traditions of knowledge and skill that enabled cultures to live less consumer-driven and thus less individually centered lives. The challenge for educational reformers is to recognize how their guiding metaphors of individualism, progress, and critical thinking are based on Western assumptions that undermine other cultural ways of knowing—including the wisdom traditions of many indigenous cultures.

The Need to Revitalize the World's Diversity of Cultural Commons. The cultural commons that exist in every community are less dependent on a money economy. They also strengthen community self-reliance, have a smaller ecological footprint, and promote the discovery of personal talents and interests that are a community's true source of wealth. The cultural commons also reduce dependence on digital technologies designed to replace workers and to expand surveillance of people's behaviors and relationships. Revitalization of the cultural commons also requires recognizing the many ways capitalism, and its guiding ideology, attempts to integrate them into the market system.

The Need to Pursue Lifestyles That Do Not Diminish the Prospects of Future Generations. This principle requires a basic shift in consciousness; one that recognizes that there are no autonomous entities such as individuals and no universal ideas. All forms of life are participants in both the cultural and natural ecologies, which means that everything is part of an emergent, relational, codependent world. This leads to recognizing the connected nature of existence—which has implications for renewing the wisdom and

New Directions for Adult and Continuing Education • DOI: 10.1002/ace

achievements of the past, and living today in ways that will enable future generations to inhabit viable environments that allow them to live morally coherent and symbolically rich lives.

The Need to Respect the Rights of Nature. This requires recognizing that species and natural systems have the right to play their role in renewing the Earth's ecosystems without being reduced in value to that of an exploitable resource.

The Cultural Roots of the Problem. All forms of education—whether tribal, institutionalized, carried on face-to-face, or based on printed texts—share a common feature. They socialize people into a task or way of thinking that adopts the values and ways of thinking of the communities into which they are being introduced. The guiding principles of an ecojustice approach to education are clearly at odds with the ways of thinking and values that are undermining the sustaining capacity of natural systems. The existing systems perpetuate socially and economically unjust relationships, and depend upon colonizing other cultures as part of a global technological and economic agenda (Merriam & Associates, 2007). Ecojustice principles, on the other hand, seek to understand the linguistic dynamics of cultural reproduction and how they can be changed. This is dependent on addressing the silences and misconceptions still carried forward in all educational programs including those in universities, colleges, K–12 schools, and community settings (Bowers, 2011a; Martusewicz, Edmundson, & Lupinacci, 2015).

Most adult educators are caught in the double bind of representing our work as on the cutting edge of progressive change while being dependent on the conceptual frameworks that we have learned from others who were unaware of the ecological crisis and how the patterns of thinking contributed to it. It is difficult for adult educators in communities and institutions to recognize the need to adopt a different paradigm than the one that underlies the individually centered industrial system of production and consumption. Real change may only come about when the current (and growing) grassroots efforts to find community-centered alternatives to consumerism leads to criticisms of how universities continue to perpetuate the dominant systems of cultural colonization (Bowers, 2011a).

Public schools and universities continue to be driven by the values and assumptions that underlie the corporate, digitized, and militarized state. Evidence that community activists may be more effective than faculty in bringing about sustainable changes in the culture can be seen in how universities now consider issues of race, class, gender, and sexual orientation as part of their curriculum. Until recently, universities reproduced the gender and racial prejudices that go back for centuries, and only changed when public pressure (including legal threats) forced them to acknowledge that they were part of the problem. This was a bottom-up driven cultural change that highlighted the reactionary nature of public schools and universities. Most members of the college-educated public have been socialized to take for granted many of the prejudices and silences of educators (Bowers, 2013).

The Difference Between Ecological and Individual Intelligence

One of the myths that still exert a hold on current thinking is the idea of individual intelligence. This myth ignores the relational nature of both natural and cultural ecologies. The continual reinforcement that individuals are the source of their own ideas, values, interpretations keeps this myth alive. The myth even survives when the evidence that should overturn this myth is presented (Bowers, 2011c).

The strongest evidence is that when a person is born into a language community, she or he is initially dependent on the vocabulary and conceptual patterns that organize their reality in terms of subject, verb, and object. If an individual relies on the vocabulary and conceptual patterns acquired from the language community, then she or he is not exercising individual intelligence. All forms of intelligence are part of a systemic, organic, and evolving relational knowledge that people experience as members of cultural groups and communities. What is distinctive about ecological intelligence is that it involves giving attention to the information being communicated within and between the other participants in the cultural and natural ecologies. Ecological intelligence is about a conscious way of thinking and being that is systemic, evolutionary, and social.

Ecological intelligence is not something that is created (Bateson, 1972; Bowers, 2011c). Everyone exercises it. I identify three levels of ecological intelligence. In Level 1, ecological intelligence is not experienced in ways that contribute to strengthening the different life sustaining ecologies—such as the well-being of the peer group, family, community, the larger culture, and the natural systems. The supposed autonomous individual, for example, exercises a limited form of ecological intelligence when she or he is initiating an activity such as speaking to someone else, passing another car on the road, or entering a crowded space of people. As everything is emergent, with information being communicated through the changes in relationships, the individual takes these changes into account by adjusting her or his behaviors in ways that lead to achieving a personal objective. The language acquired from others, the taken-for-granted beliefs that have gone unquestioned, and the larger cultural issues that are ignored, influence this expression of ecological intelligence. It is often selfish, driven by greed, prideful ignorance, and even by the desire to exploit others. In spite of these less-than-admirable traits, it is not an expression of individual autonomy. Cultural values and patterns continue to have an influence. It also needs to be pointed out that not all expressions of individually centered ecological intelligence are destructive. There are many times when people simply have to complete a task or to achieve a limited goal, which requires taking into consideration the changes occurring within the specific ecological system in which one finds oneself, such as preparing a breakfast, meeting another person as planned, or finishing a project. Yet, all of these activities still occur within a larger cultural and social context.

New Directions for Adult and Continuing Education • DOI: 10.1002/ace

Ecological intelligence is also exercised at two additional levels. The second level involves being aware of what is being communicated in a continuous cycle of ongoing relationships. Level 2 ecological intelligence helps us to move beyond the old idea of living in a world of fixed ideas and individual entities. It involves a greater awareness of the different ways in which social prejudices and various injustices are communicated and acted out. Many adult educators have become aware of the linguistic ecologies that carry forward the old stereotypes, prejudices, and patterns of marginalization, and their efforts to educate others to become aware of these patterns is evidence of ecological intelligence at the second level. Level 2 ecological intelligence might involve an understanding of the complex social relationships and apparent biases of race, gender, sexual orientation, and class evident in the world and the ways these are part of the fabric of our lives. Everyone is affected by the politics of identity and we are all part of these cultural relationships. These understandings are integral to daily experience within the emergent, relational, and co-dependent world that should now be understood as ecologies (Bowers, 2011c).

Level 3 ecological intelligence regards an understanding of all activities, expressions, and events as part of a relational ecology. It is especially important as acquiring it as a normal daily practice will contribute to reducing the levels of consumerism promoted by our hyperconsumer and industrialized culture. It involves asking how an activity helps or hinders the preservation of habitats, the use of water and nature resources. It promotes an understanding and consideration, on a daily basis, of the significant impact of the exploitation of the resources on all forms of life. What separates the exercise of Level 3 ecological intelligence from Levels 1 and 2 is that Level 3 involves awareness of how one's ideas, values, and behaviors affects the well-being of all other participants in the cultural and natural ecologies that one is co-dependent on.

And this awareness is not a matter of having an abstract commitment to sustainable living; rather it requires constant attention to how one's actions affect the behavior of the self-renewing capacity of the larger cultural and natural ecological systems. This may take the form of taking deliberate action to challenge corporate practices, or understanding that if a car is a necessity, it be energy efficient. It may take the form of buying locally rather than from foreign producers that have to ship their goods halfway around the world. It might be apparent in the development of personal skills and creative talents that reduce the need to work at a job that produces products for the consumer market and utilizes environmentally destructive technologies. As in the case of Level 2 ecological intelligence, it involves giving close attention to how the language inherited from previous generations misrepresents the co-dependency of human/nature relationships, as well as the traditions that enabled people to live less consumer-dependent lives.

Perhaps what sets Level 3 ecological intelligence off from the other levels is a very deep understanding of the cultural ecologies of all living and nonliving things. It might, for example, examine how current technologies are degrading natural systems—and the ways that the products produced by these technologies might be avoided. It may mean avoiding consuming fish now threatened by extinction. It may also mean avoiding building in environmentally sensitive areas, and using water as though it is limitless. Restoring native plants or turning green lawns into vegetable gardens are further examples of how Level 3 ecological intelligence attends to the daily practices that reduce consumerism, strengthen mutual support systems within local communities, and promote the recovery and diversity of native plants and animals. It requires a shift away from a lifestyle of self-indulgence and a money-dependent economy, and toward living lightly on the land.

Different Pathways to an Ecojustice Paradigm Shift

Addressing an ecojustice approach to educational reform also requires us to understand how we are dependent on the ways that language is used to legitimate colonizing practices. The central role of language, particularly the metaphorical nature of language, is the primary reason that making the transition to an ecojustice approach to education is dependent on community educators and professors understanding their control over language processes. The following discussion touches on the ways that language processes lead to a paradigm shift.

Language Processes. The dominant mind-set reinforced in American public schools and universities takes for granted the following: the autonomous nature of the individual and other entities, the progressive nature of change, a human-centered world, the importance of technological innovations, consumerism as the source of happiness and Euro-centric exceptionalism.

The challenge facing educators who are aware of the interconnections between the dominant mind-set and ecological changes now impacting people's lives around the world is to recognize how to bring about a change in consciousness—one that is less oriented toward consumerism and less limited by the misconceptions and silences carried forward from the past. Past notions took for granted the need to colonize other cultures in order to exploit their resources. What few educators realize, even though many are engaged in changing consciousness related to gender and racial discrimination, is that their role in socializing students in how to think about the prospects and challenges of the adult's world involves providing students with the conceptual frameworks, including the vocabularies, necessary for a postindustrial interpretation of the world. No other group in society has the same extended opportunity to provide students with the range of interpretative frameworks. Yet few educators are aware of the importance of the language processes. Only as students become aware of how their thoughts and values too often are based on the thought patterns (analogs) encoded in the vocabulary they acquired in the process of primary socialization, will they be able to recognize the ecojustice alternative lifestyles that are not only possible, but are now absolutely necessary (Bowers, 2013).

New Directions for Adult and Continuing Education • DOI: 10.1002/ace

The Linguistic Colonization of the Present by the Past. This statement suggests the range of decisions that are possibilities for teachers in all their relationships with students. That is, regardless of what aspect of culture, and its linguistic foundations, the students are interacting with, educators can always ask students to consider the history of words, which will also require a brief explanation of how the meaning of words are framed by the analogs settled on in the past. Examples of words whose meaning were framed by the analogs settled on in earlier eras, and within specific cultures, are present in every conversation and in everything students read. Whose analogs framed the meaning of "woman," "technology," "intelligence," "traditions," "winners," "wealth," and so forth? Given the cultural diversity of students in most classrooms, these words will have different meanings—which educators need to engage students in exploring.

What students are unlikely to learn outside of the classroom is that powerful evocative experiences and insights in the past serve as the basis of interpretative frameworks. These interpretative frameworks have their own supporting vocabularies that lead to recognizing different aspects of the people's life worlds. These vocabularies, as well as what is missing in them, hide awareness of other realities. Educators need to be able to explain to students how these interpretative frameworks, or root metaphors, frame their taken-for-granted patterns of thinking. These root metaphors include a human-centered world, individualism, mechanism, progress, patriarchy, economism, evolution, and now ecology. Students can learn about how these root metaphors influence how they think by identifying their supporting vocabularies as well as the vocabularies and the alternative ways of thinking that are excluded. For example, what are the different ways the root metaphor of mechanism now influences how we think about agriculture, medical practices, education, organic processes, the brain? Recognize different cultural values—including the sacred and the rights of nature?

Introducing students to the metaphorical nature of language and the role that root metaphors play in promoting the dominant interpretative frameworks in the West, as well as the role of root metaphors in other cultures, leads to other critically important issues.

If the culture's patterns of thinking are tacitly learned when learning to think and communicate with others within the language community into which one is born, then there is no such entity as an autonomous individual thinker, and no totally original ideas. The conduit (the sender/receiver) view of language, which most people take for granted, is a myth. This thinking can be demonstrated in the classroom by having adult students read a printed text, and then asking whether what is read provides any clues that the words in the sentence are metaphors and thus have a history that reproduces earlier ways of thinking—including misconceptions. This conversation with adult students should strengthen awareness of how different languages lead to different ways of understanding and constituting what is taken to be reality.

Understanding the Connections Between Print and Abstract Thinking. Our reliance on the printed word is key to our understanding. Print is based on abstract thinking, which, in turn, fails to take account of the emergent, relational, and codependent nature of most face-to-face communication. Print fosters a dependency on abstract representations that is part of every relationship with others and with the natural world (Bowers, 2014).

Educators along with their students need to discuss how the heavy reliance upon printed texts and images has undeniable advantages. However, it's essential that adults study the ecological knowledge of different cultures that rely more on oral traditions. This comparison should enable them to recognize how print has distinct characteristics that are misleading (Bowers, 2016).

The disadvantages of our heavy reliance on print include the following: (1) print provides only a surface knowledge of an event, process, and context; (2) what is encoded in print misrepresents the relational and emergent processes in the different cultural and natural ecologies; (3) print reinforces the misconception of an objective account; and (4) print is used in ways that hide that words have a history and human authorship (Bowers, 2016).

These characteristics of print need to be discussed within the contexts that are part of our experience. The aspects of local contexts, as well as the emergent, relational, and codependent nature of participating in a local ecology, that cannot be fully represented in printed accounts expose the limitations of print. What is left out of the written account? Can print fully represent the experience of the soldier in combat, for example, or the beauty of an artistic performance, or of a child's experience of poverty?

The student/educator conversation should then turn to the more complex issues of how print fosters abstract thinking by reducing awareness of the complex exchanges that take place within both the natural and cultural ecologies. Comparing the differences in what gets communicated in face-to-face relationships, and in printed accounts of behaviors will bring out the limitations of both print and data. The way in which print marginalizes awareness of the emergent and relational complexity of the behaviors within local contexts can be observed if the educator provides an explanation of the cultural patterns that need to be given special attention. That is, print reinforces abstract thinking where the printed words take on a reality that is too often divorced from everyday experiences. Ecological intelligence, on the other hand, is exercised in response to the complexity of messages communicated by others as we walk down the street, engage and in other social settings, and so on (Bowers, 2013; Goody, 1987; Ong, 1982).

Revitalizing the World's Cultural Commons. Finally, taking actions that revitalize the world's cultural commons is central to an ecojustice agenda. Surprisingly, the answer to many of the challenges we face can be found in the communities that continue to carry forward the largely nonmonetized and mutual support traditions of their ancestors. The cultural commons represent the nonmonetized and nonprivately owned knowledge, skills, and mentoring relationships that have been handed down over the generations. The cultural

New Directions for Adult and Continuing Education • DOI: 10.1002/ace

commons, in effect, represent the gift economy of how to live community-centered lives that have a smaller adverse environmental impact, and that do not require exploiting the resources of other countries. It is a gift handed down by previous generations who refined and expanded on the achievements in most areas of life. These achievements were, and continue to be, those areas of community life such as: growing, preparing, and sharing food in accordance with ethnic traditions; carrying forward traditional knowledge of healing practices; and in the varied creative arts—including the visual arts, storytelling, ceremonies, dance, and theater, poetry, in a wide range of craft knowledge and skill. These practices all carry forward patterns of reintegrating members into society. They carry the knowledge of the behavior of local ecosystems and how to utilize appropriate technologies and in the use of language that has encoded the culture's moral codes (Bowers, 2006).

Of course, not all cultures have produced cultural commons traditions free of prejudices and forms of domination. Racial, gender, caste-based, and religious prejudices have also been part the cultural commons of many cultures. However, the traditions for eliminating these practices are also part of the commons. The democratic political process, civil rights, and the systems of laws and traditions and civil liberties are also part of the cultural commons in most Western countries, with other countries (cultures) having their own narratives that guide their approach to social justice (Bowers, 2012).

Our overreliance on print-based ways of thinking, in which abstract words take on a reality independent of daily experience, prevents us from recognizing that our daily experiences are dependent on participating in the cultural commons handed down from previous generations. Our interest in the performing arts, participation in a craft tradition, favorite recipes, patterns of meta-communication about relationships, vocabularies, and sense of social justice, and games all reveal the emergent and relational world we live in, and are the examples of the ways that people rely on the commons of their cultural group.

Instead of claiming that we cannot go back, we should take a more ethnographic approach of observing all the activities, skills, knowledge, and patterns of mutual support that have been carried forward and improved on or degraded by previous generations. And we need to ask two questions. What aspects of daily life have not yet been entirely integrated into the money economy? And, what is the ecological footprint of these cultural commons activities?

A third set of questions arises that has special relevance for adult educators. As the concept of the cultural commons has not been widely discussed in education, many of the older generation may not fully recognize the ecological significance of the traditions they bring forward. The current generation is more fully dependent on the consumer-dependent lifestyle and, thus, lack the language for making explicit an awareness of the cultural commons activities they now take for granted. Here, it is important for educators to ensure that the upcoming generation learns to recognize the cultural commons in their communities, and how participating in them may be essential to both achieving food security in future years and to discovering and developing talents that will be valued by the community.

Today's adult educators need to be mediators who help adult students and others to recognize the ecologically sustainable and community strengthening traditions that should be intergenerationally renewed, as well as the traditions that should be reformed. The role of the mediator requires a deep knowledge of the cultural assumptions underlying the modernizing agenda, including the role that different languaging processes play in enclosing the cultural commons (Bowers, 2012). Enclosure is the processes of privatizing and monetizing what was previously shared in common.

The first task of the adult educator is to help other adults do a survey of the cultural commons in their community, and to recognize that the cultural commons differs within ethnic groups. Likewise, the cultural commons differs among all members of the larger society. Who are the mentors in the community, and what are the skills they practice and share with others? Do these mentors participate in networks of mutual support? What is the nature of the nonmonetized economy they practice? This first step should also include students engaging in auto-ethnographies of their own cultural commons experiences. This will avoid treating the cultural commons as an abstract idea, or as some idealized answer to the ecological crisis and the loss of employment as computers take over much of the routines of work. It will also enable students from minority cultures to recognize the importance of their own cultural commons, and the wisdom that many of its traditions carry forward.

The educator's mediating role goes beyond introducing students to the living examples of current cultural commons traditions. Mediators help students recognize how different aspects of the cultural commons are constantly undergoing changes. Expanding awareness of what would otherwise be part of the students' taken-for-granted experiences also has an important critical dimension. The mediator needs to encourage students to articulate the differences between their cultural commons and consumer-dependent experiences. Having students describe the differences in their experience is the first step toward helping them develop the communicative competence that will later be needed in resisting different forms of enclosure.

Giving students the space to reflect and articulate the differences in their experience between, for example, developing the musical skills necessary for participating in a group, and purchasing an expensive ticket to someone else's commercially hyped talent, opens the door to exploring the too often hidden influences on their own development. What are the long-term implications of learning to perform as a musician, an artist, a craftsperson, and so forth? Does this lead to a sense of community, and a sense that you have something to contribute to others? Does the consumer relationship lead to the discovery of personal talents and a sense of community, or do most consumer-based relationships lead to a sense of isolation and being valued only when engaged in a monetized relationship and activity? The whole range of cultural commons

New Directions for Adult and Continuing Education • DOI: 10.1002/ace

activities can be explored in terms of what students learn about themselves, how others perceive them, and the future relationships that might develop. The teacher's role as a mediator is not to provide ideologically driven answers to questions that students have not asked, or to limit the students' reflection on their own experiences as they move between cultural commons and consumer-based experiences.

The undermining of the world's cultural commons is occurring on two fronts. Market capitalism, in its quest to expand markets and to exploit low-cost labor and weak environmental regulations, is undermining the largely nonmonetized economies of mutual exchange and barter systems that still exist in intergenerationally connected communities throughout the world. People are gravitating toward urban areas in their search for work, which leads to the possibility that the knowledge and skills necessary for living less consumer-dependent lives may be lost in a single generation.

The intergenerational knowledge and skill passed forward largely through face-to-face communication and mentoring are now being displaced by what one might read on a computer screen. What is communicated is surface knowledge that has not been tested and refined over generations of experience. These practices promote the misconception that the basic social unit and source of intelligence is the autonomous individual, and that the world is made up of discrete facts, data, and information that can be understood separate from the cultural/environmental context from which they are taken. This ideology promotes abstract knowledge as more important than what can be learned from the face-to-face communication with people who are responding to the emergent and relational realities of everyday experience, and from the collective memories of past mistakes that must be avoided.

References

Bateson, G. (1972). *Steps to an ecology of mind.* New York, NY: Ballantine Books.

Bowers, C. A. (2006). *Revitalizing the cultural commons: Cultural and educational sites of resistance and affirmation.* New York, NY: Lexington Books.

Bowers, C. A. (2011a). *University reform in an era of global warning.* Eugene, OR: Eco-Justice Press.

Bowers, C. A. (2011b). *Educational reforms for the 21st century.* Eugene, OR: Eco-Justice Press.

Bowers, C. A. (2011c). *Perspectives on the ideas of Gregory Bateson, ecological intelligence, and educational reforms.* Eugene, OR: Eco-Justice Press.

Bowers, C. A. (2012). *The way forward: Educational reforms that focus on the cultural commons and the linguistic roots of the ecological/cultural crisis.* Eugene, OR: Eco-Justice Press.

Bowers, C. A. (2013). *In the grip of the past: Educational reforms that address what should be changed and what should be conserved.* Eugene, OR: Eco-Justice Press.

Bowers, C. A. (2014). *The false promises of the digital revolution: How computers transform education, work, and international development ways that are ecologically unsustainable.* New York, NY: Peter Lang.

Bowers, C. A. (2016). *Digital detachment: How computer culture undermines democracy.* New York, NY: Routledge.

Brown, L. R. (2008). *Plan B 3.0. Mobilizing to save civilization.* New York, NY: Norton.

Goody, J. (1987). *The interface between the written and the oral.* Cambridge, UK: Cambridge University Press.

Klein, N. (2014). *This changes everything: Capitalism vs the climate.* New York, NY: Simon & Schuster.

Martusewicz, R. A., Edmundson, J., & Lupinacci, J. (2015). *Ecojustice education: Toward diverse, democratic, and sustainable communities* (2nd ed.). New York, NY: Routledge.

Merriam, S. B., & Associates. (2007). *Non-Western perspectives on learning and knowing.* Malabar, FL: Krieger.

Ong, W. (1982). *Orality and literacy: The technologizing of the wbord.* London, UK: Methuen Press.

Orr, D. W. (2004). *Earth in mind: On education, environment and the human prospect.* Washington, DC: Island Press.

CHET A. BOWERS has written extensively on the cultural and linguistic roots of the ecological crisis. He is an American educator, author, international lecturer and environmental activist who has authored more than 25 books. Dr. Bowers is professor emeritus from Portland State University.

An ecojustice seminar, held in May 2016 at Appalachian State University in Boone, North Carolina, is described in this chapter. The ecojustice theoretical framework, the seminar class design, and our findings relative to student learning as gleaned from follow-up focus groups, reflection papers, and online discussion are reported. Seminars such as these highlight the crisis and foster knowledge about the positive human-environmental relationships necessary for changes in perceptions and behaviors.

6

Teaching Adult Ecojustice Education

Audrey M. Dentith, Onah P. Thompson

Introduction

Global warming, the alarming rise in the acidity of the world's oceans, arctic melting, the disappearance of species, and pervasive pollution all indicate that we are in an ecological crisis. Natural systems (water, farmland, forests, and fisheries) are being rapidly privatized, and the earth's resources are depleting precipitously (Bowers, 2011, 2012). Worker exploitation is rampant and corporations enjoy a seemingly unchecked power and authority over the world of work and consumption (Ford, 2009; Reich, 2011). A diminishing influence of democracy is evident and the push toward standardization and privatization is omnipresent and indicative of cultural and economic crises (Shiva, 2010). There has never been a time of greater need for an adult education focused on the environment, environmental justice, and sustainable life. Here, we advocate for an ecojustice approach to adult education. Ecojustice education is an emerging field of theory and inquiry that focuses on the cultural crisis of the environmental crisis. These scholars are concerned with the cultural practices that are shaped by the ideology underlying the industrial revolution. Hyperconsumerism and the domination of nature and all other species typify this mind-set and its accompanying practices. The cultural crisis includes an absence of regard for the ecology of all of life. Ecojustice educators maintain that the environmental crisis is a *cultural* crisis—and, as such, requires people to think and behave in ways that are less detrimental to the sustainability of life and natural ecology of earth (Martusewicz, Edmundson, & Lupinacci, 2015). Ecojustice education is also critical of the narrow focus of science in environmental studies since this does not acknowledge indigenous language, memory, imagination, values and creativity in the sustainability of the world's

NEW DIRECTIONS FOR ADULT AND CONTINUING EDUCATION, no. 153, Spring 2017 © 2017 Wiley Periodicals, Inc.
Published online in Wiley Online Library (wileyonlinelibrary.com) • DOI: 10.1002/ace.20222

people, its resources, and the environment. It is about our ways of life and how these affect what we think, do, know, and understand about the ecology of our communities.

An ecojustice framework differs from current thinking about the science of environmental education in many ways. Ecojustice education opposes the dominance of one group over another, of humans over nonhumans, or humans over nature. It also challenges current conceptions of social justice education because these theories fail to consider the ways that social justice is too often framed around middle-class values and accompanying lifestyles. These do not take into account environmental limits and the pervasive Western practices that foster hyperconsumption and excessive materialism. Ecojustice education, then, struggles against the domination of all living things, including nature and the natural world (Bowers, 2006, 2008; Martusewicz et al., 2015).

Here, we argue for new approaches to educating adults about these issues. We advocate for an education that informs people about the looming crises, yet offers ways of thinking and being in the world that focuses on positive human-environment relationships rather than on one solely concerned with the science of the environment and the deleterious effect of human activities. We believe it is much more beneficial to teach ecological issues by focusing on sustainable development through an immersion in community engagement and sustainable activities (Bowers, 2004, 2006, 2008; Dopico & Garcia-Vazquez, 2010; French, 2011; Martusewicz et al., 2015). Adults need to understand not only how they are part of the problem but about the many ways they can alter their views to help ameliorate the crisis and live sustainable lives.

Ecojustice adult education differs from environmental adult education in that ecojustice education is mainly concerned about social justice for those marginalized people most affected by climate change and pollution. Social justice issues related to the domination of nature and the natural commons (water, air, plant, and animal life) are important.

We assert that the field of adult education is perfectly posed to address this cultural crisis and to foster efforts to alter beliefs, values, and practices. In fact, we believe that adult education needs to take responsibility for addressing the (re)education of adults in a time of grave ecological crisis.

In this spirit, we sought a way for adult students to learn about ecojustice theory and related practices through an immersion class that focused on theory, issues, activism, and practice within a framework of positive human/environmental and strong cultural relationships. In this chapter, we describe our "Ecojustice Leadership Seminar," a 4-day class for doctoral students in educational leadership that was held in May 2016 at Appalachian State University in Boone, North Carolina. We describe our theoretical framework, the seminar class design and our findings relative to student learning as gleaned from follow-up focus groups, reflection papers, and online discussion. To protect the confidentiality of the participants in the program, all participant names are pseudonyms.

New Directions for Adult and Continuing Education • DOI: 10.1002/ace

Theoretical Framework of Learning

We also draw on Schon's theory of *reflection-on-action* and *reflection-in-action* to guide the design of our seminar class. Reflection-on-action refers to the process a learner engages in when she or he reflects on past actions or experiences. Reflection-in-action refers to action that the learner takes and the transpiration that occurs as a result of that reflective process (Schon, 1983). This process offered us a way to structure the process seminar participants engaged in as a result of the week-long seminar. In this way, we sought ways to promote reflection and elicit action.

Transformative learning theory informed the design of our class. For months prior to the seminar, we (the authors here) met to collectively plan activities designed to elicit significant learning among our adult students. To transform the thinking of our students, we sought to seriously challenge their values and worldviews through a reflection of perceptions and an engagement in conceptual knowledge about ecojustice education. It was our hope that students might be changed by their experience and eager to change the ways they engage with their communities, work, and personal life (Taylor, 2009). We wanted them to be deeply moved by the experience and we hoped that their beliefs, perceptions, and assumptions would be likewise challenged, too. It is through personal frames of reference that adult learners make sense of their educational experiences. It is in the disruption of these beliefs and assumptions that transformation occurs. It is not just about learning new course material, it is about the challenge to alter long-held assumptions and disruptions in the values and beliefs held by the learner (Merriam, 2004). Newman (2014) seeks a "consciousness" among learners that moves beyond self-learning to an encounter between self and the social and material worlds. Consciousness is about relationship and these are mediated by context, phenomenon, and circumstance. Learning in a transformational sense can be generated by teachers helping students to engage in the social and material world around them and to reflect on these encounters. It was our hope that the activities of the class would help students establish a different kind of relationship to the natural and human world.

Newman (2014) continues to argue that transformative learning should be apparent in dialogue. This should be collective and characterized by generative inquiry. Students might focus on some phenomenon or object of thought and through examination and inquiry into the relationship of this object and a particular individual point of view, the group comes to understand something in a wholly new way. Ideally, this kind of inquiry leads from one question to another in order to open up novel understanding.

Central Concepts of Ecojustice Education

Central concepts of ecojustice education were derived from the work of Chet Bowers who draws on Gregory Bateson to inform his work. Gregory

Bateson's notion of "double-bind" thinking was introduced to students early in the week (Bateson, 1972, 1980). This idea helped illuminate the ways Western assumptions equate higher levels of consumption with social progress––which undermines the ecological systems all life depends on. The double bind in a consumer-dependent society that goes largely unrecognized is the contradictory notion that the unabashed consumption of the world's resources brings about happiness; yet, happiness in life depends on having clean air, water, available resources, and meaningful community participation. Foremost in our thinking about one of the primary objectives of this class was to find local lifestyle alternatives that avoid the further degradation of the earth and undermine the ability of all living things to survive and thrive.

The Western use of the word *progress* also assumes that mass consumerism produces employment, and employment drives the economy. However, the continuous efforts to achieve greater efficiency and profits through further automation is actually reducing the need for workers. This is yet another double bind that current approaches to education are not addressing. As more people become marginalized by the introduction of labor-saving technologies, their self-image is undermined as is their mental health and self-satisfaction. Although these changes are systemic and beyond the control of individuals, being unemployed is now being judged as the result of personal failures. The educational challenge in ecojustice education is partly one of helping people understand a different form of wealth; that is the wealth or gift economy found by participating in the local cultural commons (Bowers, 2011, 2012).

The entitlements associated with the Western view of individualism is also the source of another double bind. The rights of individuals to pursue material products at the expense of the environment is consistently justified and reinforced through nearly all means of communication. This form of individualism is manifested in the right to produce, buy and sell without regard for the environment and/or the needs of others. As the dominant culture drives the individual to satisfy self-interest through consumerism, the knowledge and skills that represent the alternatives to a consumer-dependent lifestyle are being lost.

Ecojustice education strives for an education centered on the revitalization of the cultural commons as Bowers describes in his article in this volume. There are two types of commons—the natural or environmental and the cultural commons. The natural commons are comprised of the natural resources—air, water, land, vegetation—available for our use as inhabitants of the earth. The "cultural commons," on the other hand, are comprised of the long-term sustaining activities, tangible and abstract, that have been known for centuries. These are the life-sustaining spaces and practices, and the intergenerational knowledge and nonmonetized exchanges that have forged our social and cultural lives. The cultural commons are the practices that leave a much smaller ecological footprint, and tend to be more in harmony with the natural world than concerned with control of it. These "cultural commons" are very much alive today in all urban, rural, and suburban communities, and include the creative arts, craft knowledge, knowledge of food production and its cultivation, forms of bartering and nonmonetized systems of exchange, cultural dance and expression, oral history and storied narratives, healing and medicinal practices, and various ceremonies and games and heritage languages. In short, it is the developed patterns of mutual support and exchange that sustained communities for thousands of years. Most often, this knowledge includes responsible knowledge of the use of resources from the natural environment as well as forms of cultural customs and practices (Bowers 2006, 2011, 2012).

Class Design

Ten doctoral students in the Education Leadership program were part of the 4-day seminar course. Each day's activities are characterized by specific themes that included: *Revitalizing the Cultural Commons, Leading Local Activism, Interdisciplinary Approaches to Sustainability,* and *Sustainability and the Arts.* The course was designed such that from 9 a.m. to 5 p.m. of each day, participants journeyed through "theory," to "application," and onto "action." The interdisciplinary nature of the course featured local activists, academics, films, experiential activities and art that focused on fostering a wide-awakedness the ecological needs of contemporary communities.

Each day began with coffee, breakfast, and a chance to get focused and ready for a day of intense experience. For students to be effectively immersed in the course topics and activities, different forms of presenting the day's thematic message were adopted. These forms include a warm-up activity at the start of each day's work. Students were introduced to role-play experiences that simulated the life experiences of individuals affected by climate change around the world. We took these activities from Bigelow and Swinehart's text, *A People's Curriculum for the Earth* (2014). For example, in one scenario, we all took on the roles of invented indigenous persons who then presented their cases on the effects of climate change in their part of the world at the Indigenous Peoples' Global Summit on Climate Change. The summit was a real-life event that met in Anchorage, Alaska in April 2009, although the characters in the role play were fictitious ones designed for a role-play activity. In another activity, students were given fictitious identities and asked to rotate around the room, introducing themselves to other fictitious characters, each with a different perspective on climate change. This activity elicited much dialogue among students on the effects of climate change from the perspective of those most affected by the phenomenon. Processing the role play was followed by some discussion of the day's assigned readings (the list of readings is in the list of materials at the end of this article). A featured academic speaker (there were four in all) provided the theoretical frame for each day's thematic focus. The speakers included an internationally recognized ecojustice scholar, an artist involved in sustainability, a well-recognized sustainability scholar, and an anthropologist who works with indigenous people affected by climate change.

Table 6.1.

Dr. Chet Bowers (via SKYPE)	Dr. Greg Reck	Dr. Liz Rose	Dr. Jennifer Westerman
How the Expansion of the Digital World Reduces Social Responsibility: Implications for the Cultural Commons	*Sustainability as a Radical Social Movement: A Personal Exploration*	*Beauty and Productivity, Untethered Sisters*	*Working on Earth: Class and Environmental Justice*

To secure three of these speakers, we researched faculty's work at Appalachian State University, and, through word of mouth and review of the publications and the website, found some whose interests aligned with the goals of the seminar. Three of the speakers were from Appalachian State University. The other speaker used a web-based video content management platform to make his presentation from another location. All of these speakers contributed books or articles for students to read prior to the seminar. These readings were based on the topic of their speech. Topics and titles included the following (see Table 6.1).

In the afternoon, in order to make sense in a bodily sense, a practical application of practices related to the topic was offered. So, for example, on Day 1, *Revitalizing the Cultural Commons*, local women activists involved in the slow food and women farmers' movement were featured. On that day, one of the women farmers brought in goat cheese for all to taste in her promotion of the quality of local foods. On Day 2, *Leading Social Activism*, a panel of activists described their work challenging corporate practices related to the coal ash crisis in the Appalachian region of the Southeast. On Day 3, *Sustainability and the Arts*, in the afternoon, a local seamstress and adjunct professor of apparel design demonstrated how she practices "zero waste" garment production in her classes along with her skills at making clothing from discarded articles of clothing. During that same day, a staff person from the university led a session on mindfulness that resulted in the group creating a "found" poem. Found poetry takes existing texts, refashions and reorders them to present as new poems. It's the literary equivalent of a collage (Poets.Org, 2004). In this case, students looked through the texts required for the class in order to find words and images for a group poem. In addition to listening to others, students also engaged in bodily activities including expressive activities that spoke to their experiences and the knowledge of the presenters.

The penultimate activity of each day included films that encapsulated the theories and/or practices of the day's theme (see appendix for names of these films). For example, on the day themed around *Sustainability and the Arts*, the class watched the film, *The True Cost* (Ross & Morgan, 2015), on the apparel industry, its toxic impact on the environment and the atrocious abuse of Third World apparel workers by large clothing manufacturers.

New Directions for Adult and Continuing Education • DOI: 10.1002/ace

Finally, a wrap-up sessions at the end of each day helped students to make the connections among the various activities of the day. Through the day, all students kept a visual journal of their experiences throughout the 4-day class. These activities, in all, offered a mix of sensory experiences: seeing, hearing, touching, and tasting that guaranteed full immersion of participants in the course, it also ensured a "balanced diet" of ecologically related information. The condensed and immersive nature of the activities over the 4-day period made the class experience more visceral. Little opportunity for distraction by outside influences and a constant change of activities engaged students actively for the duration of each day.

Findings Related to Learning Among Students

Each student wrote a daily reflection in the evening and submitted these to the instructors online. Two 1-hour focus groups to gather evaluative and reflective data were held the week after the seminar ended. Additionally, the text from a 1-week online discussion was also collected. Students were finally asked to write an action plan as a result of their experience in the seminar. In our analysis of the focus groups, online discussion, and reflection papers, we identified five prominent findings that we named as follows: *Expectations Bias, Class Immersion, Emotions, Communal Time and Spirituality,* and *Action Plans.*

Expectation Bias was the frequently articulated surprise that students experienced during the class. The class was different than they expected and, in fact, exceeded their expectations. They didn't realize how little they know about the ecological crisis. Nor did they see the ways that their own practices impacted this crisis.

Sandy said the following:

> I have to say that I was pleasantly surprised about the content of the class and about how much I gained from the course. You know, sometimes you step into a class and you say "okay," I'm doing this as part of my course requirements for the program. But I stepped away feeling more inspired and that I need to do more. My learning process was a lot. I describe it as "enlightenment."

Class Immersion refers to the ways that the structure of the activities used in the class promoted learning in new ways. Karen stated, "I was not into the use of the visual journals but I found it to be a really interesting outlet through the week. I thought that was a really neat way to take notes and create something." Bradley commented on the variety of activities, "I just liked the different forms of learning. The speakers, the panels, the videos, the art. It didn't feel like a long day." Katrina also thought the different types of learning or teaching styles were very helpful.

Jared also made this remark:

> Over the course of the day, I think I moved from taking information in, hearing how it's applied, being outraged and then asking myself how am I going to do something about that.

Related to the immersion of experiential activities, Malcolm said this, "It's a different kind of engagement. It was a full body experience. Thinking about different things in different ways, in different media and it was [powerful]."

Emotions were the expressed intense feelings related to the course design and experience. Jared said with some emotion,

> I think the films were particularly confronting. They evoked first of all, outrage. And probably guilt. Then anger. Then fear. Is there anyway to ever get ourselves out of this mess?

Malcolm, "I had a fluctuation of emotions throughout the entire week but that (a film) was something that really stood out to me. I think the way the course was outlined allowed a roller coaster of emotions to naturally happen ... there was hope ... and despair."

Samuel, "The format for the class hit me in a way that no class had done. Typical class has about 3 hours a week and a lot to distract you before the next week. But, the format of the class did not create room for those emotions to die out."

Communal Time and Spirituality was evident in the moments of connection that were spiritual in nature. During the found poetry activity when all students were gathered in a circle, Brian said in the moments just after the films when the entire room was silent, he felt a form of spirituality. "There was just a beautiful space [that] opened in the silence where you could tell that everyone was thinking the same thing." Karen thought the "found" poem activity was particularly enlightening and communal, in nature. "I don't love stuff like that [group poems]. But after reading them [the poems] out loud, it was pretty exposing but also super interesting."

Andrea, "I thought there was a sort of palpable thing in the room particularly after the [movie on the coal ash crisis]. I felt like we all were moved by this movie in different ways but there was a connection between all of us ... there was a spiritual sense in the room ... it connected us all together as part of the human race."

Actions Plans refers to the articulated action plans students committed to make as a result of this course. Sandy, who is an administrator in the housing department at the university discussed the need to trouble the current practice in the department of spending more than $7,000 a month on items from Walmart. She intended to convince her colleagues that they should solicit materials from local sources even if they are more expensive. She also indicated that she would argue that they discontinue the practice of buying dozens of cheaply made T-shirts for each year's student initiative activities.

New Directions for Adult and Continuing Education • DOI: 10.1002/ace

Jared, an instructor in the College of Business, in his follow-up action, made plans to attend a weekend workshop on how to install solar panel installation for homes and businesses. He committed to learning and sharing this knowledge with colleagues and others in order to build more energy options for the community. He also vowed to showing some of the documentaries to his undergraduate business students.

Bradley, a university housing department administrators said, "I'm thinking of incorporating [these] social justice issues into our trainings." Similarly, Samuel, a community college teacher and administrator, committed to changing the class he teaches in environmental biology. "In my 15 years of teaching, I never thought that ecojustice education should be part of my science class until now. I can ... make my [class] more robust with the ideas I now have."

Conclusions and Recommendations

One area of recommendation from students regarding the design of the class described here included the need to have more time for dialogue around the topics covered by the films, talks and other activities with one another. The days were so packed with activities that students had little time to discuss among themselves. They used the lunch hour and short breaks to talk and process information.

In this class, we took up the challenge to adult students in the principles of ecojustice adult education. Little effort and initiative in adult education focuses on the environmental crisis and justice issues related to the crisis, despite the fact that many adult educators profess a commitment to social justice. Ecojustice education is ever more important today as economic globalization is forcing more and more people into poverty while natural resources are diminishing, the power of corporations continue to surge, and life-threatening pollution continues unchecked.

New "ways of being" in communities and in the world can help people everywhere to become aware of environmental issues and adopt community-centered lifestyles that thwart market and technological forces and undermine strong civic and cultural life. Building strong communities that support the preservation of the world's necessary biodiversity and fledging ecosystems can be achieved through awareness, action and determination among the world's people.

In all, the wisdom of local knowledge passed on through generations tends to embrace practices that sustain relationships between people and their environment. Relationships that advance concrete understandings of ecological wisdom are key to the sustainability of the earth. Adult educators would do well to teach ecojustice education through the incorporation of issues and examples of active engagement around these issues into their curriculum. Action plans, such as those offered up by these students, are at the core of ecojustice education for a sustainable future and the recognition of a moral effort to develop ecological intelligence and sustainable cultural life.

References

Bateson, G. (1972). *Steps to an ecology of mind.* New York, NY: Ballantine Books.
Bateson, G. (1980). *Mind and nature: A necessary unity.* New York, NY: Ballantine Books.
Bigelow, B., & Swinehart, T. (Eds.). (2014). *A people's curriculum for the earth.* Milwaukee, WI: Rethinking Schools.
Bowers, C. A. (2004). Revitalizing the commons or an individualized approach to planetary citizenship: The choice before us. *Educational Studies, 36*(1), 40–58.
Bowers, C. A. (2006). *Revitalizing the commons: Cultural and educational sites of resistance and affirmation.* New York, NY: Lexington Books.
Bowers, C. A. (2008). Rejoiner. More than being green: A response to Mike Mueller's review of transforming environmental education: Making the cultural and environmental commons the focus of educational reform. *Educational Studies, 44,* 301–306.
Bowers, C. A. (2011). *University reforms in an era of global warming.* Eugene, OR: Eco-Justice Press.
Bowers, C. A. (2012). *The way forward: Educational reforms that focus on the cultural commons and the linguistic roots of ecological/cultural crisis.* Eugene, OR: Eco-Justice Press.
Dopico, E., & Garcia-Vazquez, E. (2010). Leaving the classroom: A didactic framework for education in environmental sciences. *Culture Studies of Science Education, 6,* 311–326.
Ford, M. (2009). *The lights in the tunnel: Automation, accelerating technology and the economy of the future.* USA: Acculant.
French, J. J. (2011). Revitalizing community-based language arts curriculum and practice through ecojustice education. *New England Reading Association Journal, 47*(1), 36–43.
Martusewicz, R., Edmundson, J., & Lupinacci, J. (2015). *Ecojustice education: Toward diverse, democratic, and sustainable communities* (2nd ed.). New York, NY: Routledge.
Merriam, S. B. (2004). The role of cognitive development in Mezirow's transformational learning theory. *Adult Educational Quarterly, 55*(1), 60–68.
Newman, M. (2014). Transformative learning: Mutinous thoughts revisited. *Adult Education Quarterly, 64*(4), 345–355.
Poets.org (2004). *Found poem: Poetic form.* Retrieved from https://www.poets.org/poetsorg/text/found-poem-poetic-form
Reich, R. B. (2011). *Aftershock: The next economy and America's future.* New York, NY: Vintage Books.
Schon, D. A. (1983). *The reflective practitioner: How professionals think in action.* New York, NY: Basic Books.
Shiva, V. (2010). *Staying alive: Women, ecology and development.* Brooklyn, NY: South End Press.
Taylor, E. W. (2009). Fostering transformative learning. In J. Mezirow, E. W. Taylor, & Associates, (Eds.) *Transformative learning in practice: Insights from community, workplace, and higher education* (pp. 3–17). San Francisco, CA: Jossey-Bass.

Further Readings

Films

Beaver, P. (Producer), & Hansell, T. (Director). (2016). *After Coal* [Documentary]. Boone, NC: Center for Appalachian Studies at Appalachian State University.
Page, J. (Producer), & Page, J., & Walton, E. (Director). (1993). *Ancient Futures* [Documentary]. Berkeley, CA: International Society for Ecology & Culture (ISEC).
Ross, M. (Producer), & Morgan, A. (Director). (2015). *The True Cost* [Documentary]. Lawrenceville, GA: Life Is My Movie Entertainment Company (in association with) Untold Creative.

Salyer, R. (Producer), & Salyer, R. (Director). (2005). *Sludge* [Documentary]. Whitesburg, KY: Appalshop.

Student-Required Books and Articles

Anderson, T., & Guyas, A. S. (2012). Earth education, interbeing, and deep ecology. *Studies in Art Education, 53*(3), 223–245.
Bigelow, W., & Swinehart, T. (Eds.). (2015). *A people's curriculum for the earth*. Milwaukee, WI: Rethinking School Ltd.
Black, S. (n.d). *Fashion and sustainability*. Retrieved from the Berg Fashion Library website: http://www.bergfashionlibrary.com/page/Fashion$0020and$0020Sustainability/fashion-and-sustainability;jsessionid=BA18F72FF84681041CE5620B4783579E
Bowers, C. A. (2011). *University reform in an era of global warming*. Eugene, OR: Eco-Justice Press.
Lubarsky, S. (2012). Life-affirming beauty. In B. Tom, L. Daniel, & W. George (Eds.), *The energy reader: Overdevelopment and the delusion of endless growth*. Healdsburg, CA: Watershed Media.
Martusewicz, R. A., Edmundson, J., & Lupinacci, J. (2015). *Ecojustice education: Toward diverse, democratic and sustainable communities* (2nd ed.). New York, NY: Routledge Press.
Robertson, C., & Westerman, J. (Eds.). (2015). *Working on earth: Class and environmental justice*. Reno: University of Nevada Press.

AUDREY M. DENTITH, *PhD, is professor and director of the doctoral program at Appalachian State University in Boone, NC. She teaches courses in environmental leadership, qualitative methods, and curriculum theory. She publishes in the area of ecojustice education, women's issues, and curriculum studies.*

ONAH P. THOMPSON, *MA is a Nigerian citizen, currently living in the United States. He holds a master's degree in Environmental Politics and Policy Analysis from Appalachian State University and is currently a Public Policy doctoral student at the University of North Carolina at Charlotte.*

New Directions for Adult and Continuing Education • DOI: 10.1002/ace

7

This essay explores the concept of cultural commons and provides an illustration of a cultural commons practice from an ethnographic study of a community currency. The following section links cultural commons practices to situated and social cognitive learning theories, and then provides practical application to the higher education classroom.

Community Currencies: An Ideology of Abundance

Nancy Winfrey

For many people, small-town USA is an ideological form that cannot be quantified, but that circulates in literary, cultural, and political discourses as an authentic American space. Poll (2012) suggests that this national narrative is based on a shared commons, which he believes exists in our hearts rather than mapped as a geographical location. Small towns at the end of the 19th century, however, did exist on a map, and were tightly knit social organisms built around shared cultural and social values, local food production, traditional stories and music, and respect for their sense of place (Snell, 1992). These communities provided a vital economic and social hub for the surrounding farmland.

That local, social fabric of community responsibility and unity began to unravel as mid-20th-century modern Americans migrated to urban settings. Day-to-day commerce, once based on relationships and habit, shifted to the convenience of regional big-box centers, community care began to be outsourced as monetized professional services, and neighbors were isolated inside their homes watching television rather than socializing in common spaces during evening hours (Davies, 1998). In those days, a small-town economy was sustained by the continuing relationship between local buyer and seller, but the unrestricted choice of a market-driven economy has proven to be a forceful disruption of those relationships (Ehrenhalt, 1995). The historic commons, or community space, was gradually replaced with private property boundaries, consumer markets, and the primacy of satisfying individualized needs and wants.

Ecojustice scholar Chet Bowers (2012) is calling for a revitalization of common, community space as means not only to challenge privatization but also to engender a way of life that is less dependent on consumerism and the

New Directions for Adult and Continuing Education, no. 153, Spring 2017 © 2017 Wiley Periodicals, Inc.
Published online in Wiley Online Library (wileyonlinelibrary.com) • DOI: 10.1002/ace.20223

depletion of natural resources. Such a "cultural commons" provides a means for dialogue that enables people to study their experiences, uncover their resources, and to sustain or adapt that "way of being." This chapter explores the concept of the cultural commons, the use of community currency as a practice of the commons, and an example of community currency in Pittsboro, North Carolina. The final section links the practice of a cultural commons to situated and social cognitive learning theories, and provides practical application to the higher education classroom.

The Cultural Commons

Revitalizing the commons is not a romanticized return to earlier forms of social interaction, but it is a return to intentional care of a community, orchestrated and practiced by that community. By intentional care, I first suggest a sustainable approach to the ecology, or connections, between people and their environment. In this sense, the commons refers to the people who live in a particular bioregion and the natural resources upon which their lives depend: arable land, clean air, water, plants, and animals.

A highly mechanized, market-based economy is assumed to stimulate innovation, generate adequate employment, and provide a satisfying life for its citizens. Consumer-dependent Western economies, however, have derogated and exploited natural resources in the process of generating the goods and services that hegemonic corporations tout as necessary for that good life. Eventually, the very process of "progressive" development destroys the underlying ecological practices that are necessary to sustain it, a practice Bowers (2012) refers to as "double bind" thinking. In our quest to produce and purchase those consumer goods, we deplete the natural resources that make *any* life possible.

A revitalizing practice, on the other hand, aims to strengthen the mutual support systems within a bioregion, so that the community lives within the sustainable limits of its natural systems. This practice includes a resistance to the privatization of green spaces and water sources, so that the community can utilize those natural spaces, as opposed to enclosing that space as private property with restricted access. Rather than relying on a money-driven economy, the community can practice forms of mentoring, bartering, craftsmanship, medicinal remedies, and the growing and harvesting of food (Bowers, 2006). In addition, a revitalizing practice calls for an ecologically intelligent approach to community structures and democratic processes (Dentith, 2014).

In addition to the connections between people and their natural environment, the cultural commons also refers to the connections between the citizens themselves. Although migration to urban centers has been driven by a desire for a better life, the side effect has been a separation of people from their community culture, habits, and ritual "ways of being." Revitalizing the cultural commons begins with a discourse that shifts the ideology from a consumer market concept, one that commodifies the social order, to an alternative narrative of cooperative business that builds community resources and identity.

New Directions for Adult and Continuing Education • DOI: 10.1002/ace

Such a discourse is important because language is the fabric through which culturally specific ways of being are enacted in the community. That is, words have a history, and historical patterns of thinking can fail to accurately represent the natural or cultural ecological systems in which they are embedded (Bowers, 2001). Yet these face-to-face, collective exchanges hold the boundaries of the community and propel it forward, in either productive or harmful ways.

For example, the language of our market economy supports an ideology built on competition, hoarding and exploitation (Brueggemann, 2010; Rosenblatt, 2009). Competition exists because entitled consumerism drives a continual striving for goods and services. If these goods and services are limited, or perceived to be scarce, the perpetual dissatisfaction of striving escalates to anxiety, hoarding, and the eventual exploitation of natural resources or less powerful individuals. "Those who are living in anxiety and fear, most especially fear of scarcity," says Brueggemann, "have no time or energy for the common good" (p. 7). Language that supports an ideology of abundance, on the other hand, provides the framework necessary for cooperation, trust, and collective responsibility for the common good.

The idea of intentional care for the common good is operationalized in a cultural commons as intergenerational communication, the passing on of skills and crafts, communal music, folklore, and the renewed practice of social services which are currently outsourced to experts. McKnight and Block (2012) describe the process as a "citizen economy" when the community creates a context where local capacities, resources, and talents are valued over market-dictated, monetized indicators of success and satisfaction. These practices reinforce the community's identity as one of abundant resources in terms of time, energy, experience, good ideas and collective responsibility. This way of being can support the work necessary to locate and integrate the specific resources within the community, and to do so in a mutually dependent, sustainable fashion.

Community Currencies

One way to foster a revitalization of cultural commons practices is the creation of a local currency, roughly 200 of which have been launched in the United States over the past 20 years (Collom, 2011). Some of those community currency systems are motivated by oppositional ideology, and combine the use of local currency with sustained protest or disruptive behavior toward capitalistic economies. Other systems are conceived as alternative social movements, often created in conjunction with multiple community development practices. Lietaer (2001) points out that the motivation for a community currency is likely less about economics than about fostering community spirit, identity, or collective self-reliance.

In terms of economics, the health of a community is measured by the circulation of money, counting the number of transactions made until a dollar

New Directions for Adult and Continuing Education • DOI: 10.1002/ace

leaves that community. The more transactions made within the community, the higher the circulation number and the greater the stability of that local economy. Glover (2009) describes the circulation of money as a process of recycling wealth within a bioregion and as a way to strengthen that region. Economic development, however, is traditionally controlled by distant elites who are focused on financial gain more than concern for natural resources or care for the common good of local citizens. When average citizens come together to create local industries and community development programs, they increase circulation, but eventually those dollars migrate out to national or multinational corporations. A local currency, however, keeps circulation totally within the local economy, as that tender is only accepted within the boundaries set by the community. Anchoring local commerce in this way, labor and environmental standards can plausibly be raised with confidence that businesses will adapt rather than flee to off shore production facilities (Schuman, 2002). In other words, what is good for the business cannot be uncoupled from what is good for the community.

The Pittsboro Plenty

An example of a community currency can be found in Pittsboro, North Carolina, a rural town of nearly 4,000 people and the governmental seat of Chatham County. In 2002, a group of active, forward thinking citizens launched the Piedmont Local EcoNomy Tender, or "Plenty." Under the organization of the Plenty Currency Cooperative, they intended to support the local economy on three levels. First, the use of Plentys would safeguard local jobs and make small-scale production of goods and services viable. Keeping circulation within the community would reduce dependency on generic big-box stores and distribute wealth more evenly among local business owners. Second, use of the Plenty would increase awareness of local resources, the impact of consumption habits, and reduce packaging, shipping materials and the fuel needed to transport goods and services from distant locations. Thirdly, the use of Plentys would support the community values of neighborliness, generosity, and self-reliance as they were traded in face-to-face retail interactions. (L. Estill, personal communication, October 29, 2013). These three purposeful outcomes exemplify sustainable cultural commons practices.

In downtown Pittsboro, on the circle street surrounding the county courthouse, is the local Capital Bank, where Plentys can be exchanged for Federal Reserve notes, or U.S. dollars. The exchange rate is one-to-one, and Plentys come in the standard denomination of 1P, 5P, 10P, 20P, and 50P. The notes were professionally designed with beautiful watercolor images that honor the landmarks, wildlife, and cultural attributes of the region. On the bottom of each bill is the slogan "In Each Other We Trust," which refers to neighbors, the community as a whole, and in the community leaders. Trust is in fact the basis of value for any currency, as Federal Reserve notes have not been backed by gold or silver since 1933 (Estill, 2008; Lietaer, 2001).

New Directions for Adult and Continuing Education • DOI: 10.1002/ace

Currently $16,000 worth of Plentys have been issued in Pittsboro, although not all of them are in circulation. In the spring of 2009, the Pittsboro Plenty was nationally featured by CNN and USA Today, and that media exposure increased the number of community merchants welcoming Plentys. Public opinion was highly in favor of a community currency. Since that time the circulation has slowed and Glover (2009) suggests that without a full-time networker to promote the Plenty, external events or circumstances are likely continually influence the ebb and flow of a volunteer-driven community practice.

A Realist Ethnographical View

Observations for this ethnographic study of the Pittsboro Plenty were conducted as an onlooker, rather than as a participant. In addition to observation, data were collected from interviews with community residents and business owners. Relevant literature included a book written by Pittsboro resident and Plenty advocate Lyle Estill, entitled *Small is Possible: Life in a Local Economy*. The story is viewed here through the lens of a realist ethnographer. The realism distinction is in reference to the objective, third-party stance of the researcher in providing a description of the situation. Ethnography is an appropriate method because Pittsboro residents who use the Plenty are a culture-sharing group; sharing a language (Cresswell, 2013) and certain behaviors associated with the use of a community currency. Jensen and Kaplan (2008) uses the term "human ecology" to describe the small interactions between neighbors that create an intricate structure to support community life in much the same way as topsoil supports our biological existence. Those interactions are negotiations toward a shared responsibility for the common good, in local resident Lyle Estill's words, the "little transactions amongst ourselves that form the fiber of a sustainable community" (Estill, 2008, p. 191).

As an example, when Estill opened a business downtown that was bordered by a long brick wall, he and local artist Clyde Jones decided it was ugly.

> We decided on a whim that if I were to get the wall painted blue, and provide some scaffolding, he would paint a mural on it. Which we did. Tami rounded up school children, the local hardware store's paint vendor donated the paint, and off we went. The mural went up in fine fashion. Someone called the police, thinking is was a violation of the local sign ordinance, but when the chief of police came to inspect, he thought it looked fine to him. (Estill, 2008, p. 25)

Seyfang (2001) speaks to a shared culture by noting that a community currency not only provides a practical alternative to value regimes and capitalistic logic but also builds a supportive social network of people who share values and ideals, defining how they see themselves as a community, and how they engage with one another.

New Directions for Adult and Continuing Education • DOI: 10.1002/ace

The Pittsboro Plenty also created an economic network by requiring an initial "membership" process of exchanging $15 for five Plentys. For business owners and entrepreneurs, those five Plentys came with inclusion in both a print and online directory of local products and services. Each member could specify the percentage of Plentys allowed per business transaction. When the biodiesel co-op needed to rewire their physical plant, they found an electrician in the directory who accepted Plentys for 10% of her services. In this way circulation of the community currency expanded. She added a new customer because of her use of Plentys and the co-op was pleased that their money was spent locally.

The strength of this social order grounded in relationships began as simple conversation between friends around a kitchen table. As local business grew and the Plenty continued to circulate within community boundaries, the conversation was shaping a new narrative of interdependence and sustainable living. Lyle Estill, owner of Piedmont Biofuels, recounted the early planning of a Pittsboro music festival, where a local resident's "contagious energy" brought the project to fruition. "You guys look after the fuel," he said to Estill, [and] "we'll take care of the entertainment." Estill shared that "simple remark had a profound impact on me … it dawned on me that if we could each take our part of the load, we could form a self-reliant community that could exist without the need for massive external inputs" (Estill, 2008, p. 190).

Now, 12 years later, the festival spans 4 days of music with 50 bands, local food and art, dancing, and community awareness projects. The festival is supported by the Shakori Hills Community Arts Center, which hosts cultural events, maintains an 8,800-square-foot organic community garden, and teaches environmental awareness and sustainable living practices. Their longest running program, *Roots in the Schools* (RiS), brings musicians and artists into local schools. At a time when public schools are cutting music and art budgets, RiS provides the cultural commons practice of passing on local knowledge to the next generation of citizens.

Another result of a strong social and economic fabric of relationship is the Chatham Marketplace, a locally owned and operated grocery store in what had been an abandoned textile mill. An early adopter of the community currency, the Marketplace created a business plan based on local buying and selling. Providing a local marketplace in a global economy is no small task, however, and Estill reflects that "the story of Chatham Marketplace is a remarkable tale of one woman's vision, which became a group endeavor, which is an ongoing community work-in-progress" (Estill, 2008, p. 101).

The Cultural Commons and Adult Learning Theory

Brookfield (2005) conceives of theory as simply a set of explanations intended to make sense of some aspect of the world. To understand the process of creating and disseminating a new narrative of abundance within the Pittsboro community, the theories of situated and social cognitive learning are

New Directions for Adult and Continuing Education • DOI: 10.1002/ace

helpful. These two theories are explored in relation to the cultural commons as follows.

The Cultural Commons and Situated Learning

An argument could be made for a link between a cultural commons practice, such as the Pittsboro Plenty, and "communities of practice" as described by Jean Lave in her theory of situated learning (Lave, 1991). Wenger, McDermott, and Snyder (2002) make the connection themselves by applying their principles of successful communities of practice to a local community initiative. Those principles are natural evolution, distributed leadership, participation from a range of perspectives, formal and informal process and structures, value, and a stable, existing culture from which to work. There is evidence of all these principles in the Pittsboro Plenty initiative.

Natural evolution results from a process of iterative action-reflection cycles, which in the case of the Plenty began with the conversation of neighbors around Estill's kitchen table, and grew into the first issue of a community currency. With time, experience, and continued reflective conversation, the currency was adjusted and reissued. In the second phase, the denominations of the Plenty were adjusted to match Federal Reserve notes, and the base of distribution shifted from the nearby town of Carrboro to Pittsboro. Distributed leadership and formal/informal process are also intertwined in the life of the Plenty. The currency was launched as a formal membership cooperative, and then later reorganized as an initiative under the umbrella of the Abundance Foundation, a local nonprofit. Promotion of the currency has been an informal process, a grassroots effort from those citizens who valued the alternative currency option. There has always been a small group of committed citizens driving the project, as opposed to the vision, or full-time effort, of a single individual.

The third element reflective of a community of practice is the participation of individuals with a broad range of perspectives. This element is evidenced in the different businesses that accept Plentys. Angelina's Greek Kitchen, the Chatham Marketplace Food Co-Op, and Piedmont Biofuels are among the long-standing supporters of the Plenty. The use of a community currency has not effectively transitioned from the alternative subculture to the mainstream, however, and this has limited the visibility and success of the Plenty (Estill, 2008). In an informal interview of selected business owners on the main street, there was a continuum from not knowing of the Plenty, to being aware but not accepting it as payment, to an eagerness to support its use as a community currency.

Value, a fourth community of practice principle, is a meaningful return on investment for each individual, and also as collective output. The value of maintaining a community currency is seen in the economic health of a community, as well as in the relationships of those who participate in trading Plentys, as illustrated earlier. Environmental responsibility and community self-reliance also develop as more citizens learn about alternative currencies and the connections between ecological intelligence and a stable community economy. Value is a socially constructed principle, and is developed from the starting point of an existing culture. This is the final community of practice principle; that shifting the collective framework of a community begins with a small subculture. In the case of the Plenty, a small group of citizens are shifting their "way of being" in the community to a more ecologically sound, sustainable lifestyle (L. Estill, personal communication, October 29, 2013). In order to be successful, that lifestyle necessarily draws in other individuals, businesses, and community partnerships, and that increased awareness and cooperation will contribute to a more healthy community. This behavior is the manifestation of Bower's (2012) definition of a cultural commons—the intrapersonal connections between people and between those people and the bioregion that sustains their community.

In the same way that situated learning theory is in fact "situated" in real world scenarios and problems, the use of a community currency in Pittsboro is also contained within a larger, collective movement toward a healthy, ecologically intelligent town. "Even when imaginative rural and community development programs have been able to stabilize local economies," says Davies, "the potential for a downward spiral is always lurking nearby" (Davies, 1998, p. 194). In view of that reality, the fledgling Plenty is nested in other more robust initiatives. For example, Pittsboro hosts an art collaborative, music festival, impromptu concerts, and a commercial biodiesel facility that fuels 400 families with alternative energy. There is a food co-op, a slow money loan program and an educational partnership with the local community college. There are online bloggers, local news publications and published authors who work together to unpack and publicize the principles of sustainable community living. These interdependent efforts support a network of community wealth that is ecologically intelligent and sustainable, rather than dependent on a system designed to make costs public while privatizing profits.

The Cultural Commons and Social Cognitive Theory

The quality of the learning in situated learning, however, is dependent on the quality of the relationships among members of the community. Newcomers learn from those who are more closely connected, and tacit knowledge becomes explicit as shared experience evolves into a local epistemology. A primary tenet of situated learning is that collaborative social interaction advances the construction of knowledge, as opposed to knowledge being passed down in a formal, hierarchal manner. Collaboration, however, is no small task in a society that places a premium on individualism

New Directions for Adult and Continuing Education • DOI: 10.1002/ace

and competitive striving for goods and services that are perceived to be limited.

Bandura's (1986) social learning theory pairs well with situated learning concepts in that the behavior that is observed and imitated in a community of practice is dependent on cognitive processes. That is, the gap between observation and imitation is mitigated by a conscious decision to engage as a community in collaborative practices (Merriam, Caffarella, & Baumgartner, 2007). Community conceived as a connection of people and their environment provides the setting for the interactive model of Bandura's theory; behavior is a function of the interaction of an individual and his environment, and the reciprocal influence of the environment shapes the learning of the individual. Thus, the three components of the model—individual, environment, and learning—have the potential to create a collaborative community of practice where an ideology of abundance prevails. On the other hand, those three components can manifest the double bind ideology of progress as a spiral that fragments the community into individualism and competition, without regard for the bioregion that sustains them.

The rise and fall of the Pittsboro Plenty could reflect Bandura's view of self-efficacy within his social cognitive theory. Self-efficacy refers to a personal assessment of competence engaging in a particular environment. If individuals feel confident using Plentys in their local transactions, that confidence influences the community. When CNN was in town reporting on the local currency, collective self-efficacy was high, and trading increased. When one resident complained that a particular business did not accept Plentys, concern spread that other businesses would follow suit and the confidence of the collective diminished and indeed, trading decreased (L. Estill, personal communication, October 29, 2013).

Connecting the Classroom to the Cultural Commons

Brookfield and Holst (2011) advocate for a return to the roots of adult education as a practice necessarily embedded with moral, social, or political purpose and essential to creating and sustaining economic and political democracy. It is about teaching people to resist dominant, hegemonic ideology. Amsler (2013) laments that adult higher education has "domesticated the radical potential of the traditions from which it grew" and calls for a broad conceptualization of critical pedagogy as a way of life, rather than simply a method for teaching and learning. In the higher education classroom, getting students to think critically does not imply setting forth a higher order form of reasoning, but rather adding a critical dimension to their existing process of meaning making, their way of life. Daily practices are embedded in a theoretical reading of experience, where critical inquiry can explore the underlying taken-for-granted beliefs and language. In this way, academic theory is not disconnected from individual, and ultimately community life, but in fact informs it. The link between abstract

New Directions for Adult and Continuing Education • DOI: 10.1002/ace

conceptualization in the classroom and experience with ecojustice issues is addressed here in terms of leadership and partnership.

Leadership

The process of mediating between experiential knowledge and theoretical concepts begins with the educator's own practice of meaning making and application of new understanding. That is, utilizing theory to both analyze experience in context and enable subsequent action; a critical process that "involves people in theorizing their experience: they stand back from it and reorder it, using concepts like power, conflict, structure, values, and choice" (Foley, 1999, p. 64). When educators are navigating their own assumptions—of Foley's concepts, for example—and providing full disclosure of their position and intentionality in the classroom, they set a tone of authenticity that enables students to engage in a similar process of critical inquiry (Winfrey, 2016). Amsler (2013) suggests that, in addition to modeling process, educators should view the content they provide not as authoritative answers but as a "rich archive of collective problem-posing theorization and experience that we can draw on and contribute to through our own intellectual and political projects" (p. 67). This view, she believes will move education beyond critique of existing systemic ecojustice issues toward a "process of creating something new—a piece of work, a relationship, a sense of self, a feeling, a space, an imaginary, a possibility" (p. 79).

Analyzing experience requires "intense thinking and listening" as the general and then particular elements of experience are unraveled and coupled with theoretical concepts (Preskill & Brookfield, 2009). Creating a time and space for collective, critical reflection in academic settings requires competence on the part of the educator to institute democratic dialogue parameters and the principles of safe space. Utilizing recent exploration into ecojustice initiatives, such as Dentith's 2014 documentary on the cultural commons, in conjunction with formal academic courses (see Dentith & Thompson, Chapter 6, this volume), could generate Amsler's sense of "possibility" as students begin to view themselves as knowledge producers and agents of change (Choudry, 2015).

Partnership

If formal and nonformal learning can be considered on a continuum, the incidental, informal experience of a student can be analyzed and validated alongside a conceptual understanding of the theories within the adult learning discipline. To view critical pedagogy as a "way of life," as suggested by Amsler, both the classroom and the community must be engaged by an ecojustice curriculum. Choudry (2015) explains that "rather than considering movements, learning and education, organizing, knowledge production, and activist research as separate categories, I [believe] these are dialectically linked"

(p. 22). The everyday discourse and activity of people creates, sustains, and remakes social relations. In order to think differently, more ethically and deeply about the cultural foundations of the problems we face, educators must tie relevant, interdisciplinary, community-based learning projects to the curriculum (Martusewicz, Edmundson, & Lupinacci, 2011). What are the cultural roots of the social and ecological problems manifest in the local community? Where does the student, as a citizen of that community, find a public discourse that is meaningful? What are the connections between his personal ethics, his own actions, the academic content, the particulars of the community, and the processes in which people engage each other to create that complex social fabric? This sort of "practical-intellectual politics" (Amsler, 2013) can take many forms, and some will be more possible than others, but the movement from the classroom to emerging spaces of collective action in the community will empower the discourse that links analysis and critique with sustainable living.

Conclusion

Although the cultural commons initiative studied in this essay began within a subculture of the Pittsboro community, the use of the community currency, and the ideology of sustainable living that undergirds that initiate, are developing democratically and spreading organically over time. As such, progress is slow and often messy. Aldo Leopold, one of the foremost conservationists of the last century, believed that the most profound aspects of human experience are linked to a deep understanding of the natural world—that a responsible land ethic is an intellectual as well as emotional human undertaking. His often quoted guideline for sustainable democratic decision making is that "A thing is right when it tends to preserve the integrity, stability, and beauty of the biotic community. It is wrong when it tends otherwise" (Leopold, 1949, p. 224). The citizens of Pittsboro are engaged in the collective, intellectual, emotional, critical inquiry and action that is generating a new narrative of abundance and environmental care. For that community, it is a "right thing."

In addition, living within the limits of natural systems requires less time spent working to pay for monetized goods and services, and affords more opportunity to engage in activities that sustain a sense of abundance within the community (Bowers, 2001). Estill (2008) reflects that "our community has never been stronger," explaining:

Ten years ago, if I needed a ride to town, I would have found myself stranded in the woods.... Today there are more people "looking after" one another than ever before.... Whether you need the garden watered, or a pet cared for, or a safe place to heal, or a ride to town, these woods have never been so full of opportunities ... full of so many people who are on life's big adventure. (p. 215)

Ultimately, the cultural commons serves as the sum of all a community owns together—the narrative of abundant resources leveraged for their common good—and which they must pass on, undiminished, to the future (Barnes, 2003).

References

Amsler, S. (2013). Criticality, pedagogy and the promises of radical democratic education. In S. Cowden (Ed.), *Critical pedagogy in, against, and beyond the university* (pp. 62–84). Huntingdon, UK: Bloomsbury Academic Press.

Bandura, A. (1986). *Social foundations of thought and action: A social cognitive theory.* Englewood Cliffs, NJ: Prentice Hall.

Barnes, P. (2003, October). *Capitalism, the commons, and divine right.* Symposium conducted at the Twenty-third Annual E. F. Schumacher Lectures, Stockbridge, MA.

Bowers, C. A. (2001). How language limits our understanding of environmental education. *Environmental Education Research, 7*(2), 141–151.

Bowers, C. A. (2006). *Revitalizing the cultural commons: Cultural and educational sites of resistance and affirmation.* Landham, MD: Lexington Books.

Bowers, C. A. (2012). *The way forward: Educational reforms that focus on the cultural commons and the linguistic roots of the ecological/cultural crisis.* Eugene, OR: Eco-Justice Press.

Brookfield, S. (2005). *The power of critical theory: Liberating adult learning and teaching.* San Francisco, CA: Wiley.

Brookfield, S., & Holst, J. (2011). *Radicalizing learning.* San Francisco, CA: Jossey-Bass.

Brueggemann, W. (2010). *Journey to the common good.* Louisville, KY: Westminster Press.

Choudry, A. (2015). *Learning activism.* Toronto, Canada: University of Toronto Press.

Collom, E. (2011). Motivations and differential participation in a community currency system: The dynamics within a local social movement organization. *Sociological Forum, 26*(1), 144–168.

Cresswell, J. (2013). *Qualitative inquiry and research design: Choosing between five approaches.* Los Angeles, CA: Sage.

Davies, R. O. (1998). *Main street blues: The decline of small-town America.* Columbus: Ohio State University Press.

Dentith, A. (Producer). (2014). *The way forward: Revitalizing the cultural commons in ecojustice work.* Available from https://www.youtube.com/watch?v=8PvKnXY7r_E

Ehrenhalt, A. (1995). *The lost city: The forgotten virtues of community in America.* New York, NY: Basic Books.

Estill, L. (2008). *Small is possible: Life in a local economy.* Gabriola Island, Canada: New Society.

Foley, G. (1999). *Learning in social action.* New York, NY: St. Martin's Press.

Glover, P. (2009). *A recipe for successful community currency* [Web log post]. Retrieved from http://www.paulglover.org/

Jensen, D., & Kaplan, J. (2008). *Change everything now.* Great Barrington, MA: Orion Press.

Lave, J. (1991). Situating learning in communities of practice. *Perspectives on socially shared cognition, 2,* 63–82.

Leopold, A. (1949). *A sand county almanac.* New York, NY: Oxford University Press.

Lietaer, B.A. (2001). *Community currencies: A new tool for the 21st century.* Retrieved from http://transaction.net/money/cc/cc01.html

Martusewicz, R., Edmundson, J., & Lupinacci, J. (2011). *Ecojustice education: Toward diverse, democratic, and sustainable communities.* New York, NY: Routledge Press.

McKnight, J., & Block, P. (2012). *The abundant community: Awakening the power of families and neighborhoods.* San Francisco, CA: Berrett-Koehler.

Merriam, S., Caffarella, R., & Baumgartner, L. (2007). *Learning in adulthood: A comprehensive guide.* San Francisco, CA: Jossey-Bass.

Poll, R. (2012). *Main street and empire: The fictional small town in the age of globalization.* Piscataway, NJ: Rutgers University Press.

Preskill, S., & Brookfield, S. (2009). *Learning as a way of leading: Lessons from the struggle for social justice.* San Francisco, CA: Wiley.

Rosenblatt, A. (2009). (Re)localization: An exploration in local currencies. *Community Economics, 142,* 58–59.

Seyfang, G. (2001). Community currencies: Small change for a green economy. *Environment and Planning, 33,* 975–996.

Schuman, M. (2002, January). *Going local: New opportunities for community economics.* Symposium conducted at the Community Land Trust of the Southern Berkshires Annual Meeting, great Barrington, MA.

Snell, M. B. (1992). The art of place: An interview with Wendell Berry. *New Perspectives Quarterly, 9,* 29–34.

Wenger, E., McDermott, R., & Snyder, W. (2002). *Cultivating communities of practice.* Boston, MA: Harvard Business School Press.

Winfrey, N. (2016). Where do we go from here? *Adult Learning, 27*(3), 131–133.

NANCY WINFREY, PhD, has been educating adults for 20 years in corporate and nonprofit settings. She is also an experienced instructional designer. Her current research interest is the critical theory underpinning experiential learning, action research, and group processes.

New Directions for Adult and Continuing Education • DOI: 10.1002/ace

8

This chapter examines the revitalization of the cultural commons in one Massachusetts community. The adult learning theory of situated cognition, specifically communities of practice and cognitive apprenticeship, provides a lens through which to better understand how knowledge sharing can effectively promote localization in an effort to mitigate climate change.

Transition Framingham: The Cultural Commons in Action

Emily Kearns Burke

Climate change is a grave consequence to those practices that characterize our modern, industrialized world. Climate change increases in severity every day (United States Environmental Protection Agency, 2013). It is a direct result of the planet's rising temperature, which has increased by 1.4°F over the past 100 years, and is estimated to rise another 2 to 11.5°F over the next century. What may appear to be small increases in the average temperature of the planet will ultimately translate into huge and potentially threatening shifts in climate and weather. While even more severe changes are projected to come, our oceans are warming; ice caps are rapidly melting causing sea levels to rise. In addition, changes in rainfall patterns are causing either extreme flooding or devastating drought in many parts of the world. As is widely acknowledged, human activity is the culprit as the burning of fossil fuels and associated industrial practices have released large amounts of greenhouse gases that have trapped energy in the atmosphere and caused the Earth to warm. And yet humans will suffer the consequences of their own actions, as climate change threatens population growth, nutritional health, and food supplies while simultaneously maintaining poverty and disadvantage in already depleted regions (McMichael, 2013).

As citizens face an uncertain environmental future, the need for communities to learn and band together with shared goals for sustainability and resilience has increased (Hopkins, 2008). Adult education is more critical than ever before, able to serve as a way to generate knowledge, build awareness, and, ultimately, act as a catalyst for change. According to the United States Environmental Protection Agency (2013), it is not too late to make a substantial impact on future climate change and its effects. Although changes will be

NEW DIRECTIONS FOR ADULT AND CONTINUING EDUCATION, no. 153, Spring 2017 © 2017 Wiley Periodicals, Inc.
Published online in Wiley Online Library (wileyonlinelibrary.com) • DOI: 10.1002/ace.20224

required at all levels and within all societies, small communities of committed people can affect change. Moreover, as the environmental crisis increases, the need to find new ways to survive and thrive in the midst of environmental disaster is crucial. In this chapter, I define and discuss the importance of the cultural commons in the context of adult learning. I present the Transition Movement and one of its local divisions, Transition Framingham, as examples of the commons and its efforts to combat the environmental crisis. Finally, I offer an analysis of the learning that is evident in these communities and the role that adult educators can play in fostering and enhancing these efforts.

The Cultural Commons

Humans need to move away from a dependence on fossil fuel production to live in communities that are less reliant on patterns of consumption and more reliant on patterns of mutual support and an unwavering commitment to decreasing one's toxic and carbon impact. One way that some environmental scholars and activists believe we can achieve these goals is through the revitalization of the cultural commons. The cultural commons, which has existed since the beginning of mankind, is key to community resiliency and survival as the industrial/consumer culture begins to collapse and the Earth's temperature rises (Bowers, 2013).

The cultural commons is the activities, knowledge, skills, and patterns, which sustain daily life by encouraging local decision making that benefits the whole of a community rather than promoting self-interest, competition, and profit. It is unique to each community, but exists everywhere. The cultural commons can be found in community healing practices, food preparation and sharing, the arts, the building of dwellings, the caring of animals, and other practices that minimize human impact on the planet. These practices focus on the central tenets of heritage and relationship, exemplified by the community's value of intergenerational knowledge and mentoring (Bowers, 2013). Rather than promoting enclosure, where these traditional practices are turned into commodities for monetary gain, the commons seeks to provide an alternative to the consumer-driven lifestyle that has become commonplace in modern societies (Bowers, 2009).

While the cultural commons is, and has been, present in every community, it is only recently that groups of individuals have purposely resurrected sustaining practices from the past in a conscious effort to revitalize the commons as a method of counteracting the mainstream industrial, consumer-driven, and isolating messages of society (Bowers, 2013). An example of this purposeful commitment to socially and environmentally responsible actions and the revitalization of practices that encourage a move toward strong communities, less consumption, and a lesser dependency on fossil fuel production is the Transition Movement, which was originally founded by Rob Hopkins in the early 2000s.

New Directions for Adult and Continuing Education • DOI: 10.1002/ace

The Transition Movement

The Transition Movement is designed around grassroots community initiatives that aim to foster community resilience in the face of such challenges as peak oil, climate change, and the economic crisis (Hopkins & Lipman, 2009). In this context, resilience is defined as the ability of a system ranging from individuals to entire economies to preserve its ability to operate and withstand change and shocks from outside systems (Hopkins, 2008). Transition initiatives seek to alleviate these merging global challenges by engaging communities in local citizen-led education, action, and multistakeholder planning to discourage reliance and promote systemic resilience.

An underlying philosophy of the Transition Movement focuses on the idea that a proactive response to the existing and anticipated environmental crises can be positive and hopeful, rather than fearful and guilt-ridden (Hopkins, 2008). It is the vision of the Transition Movement that environmental campaigning and education can be inspirational, enthusiastic, and enjoyable by being proactive instead of reactive; it is possible to transform future energy consumption in ways that create a way of life that is superior to our current existence.

The Transition model has six distinctive principles that undergird its approach (Hopkins, 2008). These six principles are visioning, inclusion, awareness-raising, resilience, psychological insights, and credible and appropriate solutions. Visioning is the idea that growth and change within a community is only possible when the end result can be imagined. It is a clear picture of the desired outcome that provides direction and motivation. The principle of inclusion suggests that dialogue and the coming together of different groups of people representing different interests in the community are critical to success. If like-minded individuals, or only those from specific sectors of the community, join the movement then it is unlikely that a true transition will occur given the scale of the peak oil crisis and climate change. Awareness-raising, the third principle in the Transition Movement, posits that with the mixed messages delivered by the media, it is necessary to share information regarding Earth's ecological crises, rather than assume prior knowledge. The principle of resilience, as stated earlier, is the ability of a community to withstand outside change by creating opportunities for sustainability through locally sourced avenues. Psychological insights is a principle that recognizes that human feelings of powerlessness and isolation in the face of peak oil and climate change are fundamental barriers to engagement that prohibit action and involvement. Focusing on the positive aspects of change, recognizing successful prior actions for the cause, and creating a safe space for people to gather to work toward local sustainability provide opportunities to boost psychological morale. The final principle in the Transition initiative is credible and appropriate solutions, meaning that individuals and communities must be provided with opportunities to effect change at an appropriate scale that can include things individuals can do in their own homes as well as larger solutions that can be accomplished as a community.

Hopkins' (2008) Transition principles developed from work that the permaculture designer had done with students at Kinsale Further Education College in Ireland to adapt existing programs of energy production, health, education, economy, and agriculture in order decrease oil dependence and promote a sustainable future for the community. The idea was adopted by the town of Kinsale, quickly expanded to Hopkins' hometown of Totnes, England, which became the first Transition Town, and then spread across the world. Now the Transition program is in 14 countries, including the United States.

The international movement focuses on educating participants and outside community members about the benefits of local production of food, alternative systems of transportation, energy conservation of homes and businesses, reusing, recycling, and repairing items rather than throwing them away (Hopkins, 2008). This sharing of skills and knowledge is done intergenerationally through social events like lectures, films, and the arts, and through both formal and informal mentoring relationships.

Transition and Adult Learning

The Transition Movement is by no means an isolated idea, or the first of its kind. The concept of economic localization, promoted by groups like the Business Alliance for Local Living Economies (Business Alliance for Local Living Economies, 2012) and grassroots organizers such as Helena Norberg-Hodge (2010) have championed the need to contain economic activity within local geographic areas in order to foster sustainable, cohesive communities and decrease the wealth gap between rich and poor. These political ideologies argue against economic globalization and consumption in favor of regional resources, supportive social connections, and collaboration among local businesses.

Yet even before the Transition or localization movements were born, Eduard Lindeman, an early adult-learning theorist, advocated for the importance of adult collaboration and the informal exchange of ideas as an avenue of social change (Brookfield, 1984). Lindeman believed the essential purpose of adult learning was to aid individuals as they were confronted with critical social and political issues (Lindeman, 1937). Lindeman, and other adult-learning advocates like Myles Horton, argued that adults learn through collaborative, nonauthoritarian exchanges that develop community, fuel engagement, and encourage social change (Brookfield, 1984).

The influences of adult educators such as Edward Lindeman and Myles Horton can be found in examples such as the Transition Movement in which the importance of adult collaboration and the informal exchange of ideas are the paths to social change. These ideals have spread throughout the world and into local communities, including Framingham, Massachusetts where the Transition Movement continues to grow.

New Directions for Adult and Continuing Education • DOI: 10.1002/ace

Transition Framingham

Founded in 2011 on Hopkins' principles of the Transition Movement, Transition Framingham, located in the state of Massachusetts, offers an example of this movement in practice. It is comprised of more than a dozen core members who are dedicated to sustainability and resilience in their own town as well as hundreds of residents on their mailing lists who participate in Transition Framingham-sponsored events (retrieved from http://transitionframingham.org/about, 2015). Transition Framingham promotes these values by forming work groups around recycling, permaculture, renewable energy, and community education while also creating town-wide awareness through small community projects focused on gardening and farming, food preparation and preservation, as well as bike clinics and other environmentally sound transportation initiatives (J. Knapp-Cordes, personal communication, October 28, 2013).

Janice Knapp-Cordes, one of the founding members of Transition Framingham, became involved with the group after seeing a film at the public library on climate change presented by advocates of the Transition Movement. Subsequently, Knapp-Cordes scheduled a showing of the film at her church and from there a group formed, ready to create Transition Framingham. The growth of the group was slow, and in the first year, the members were able to organize a locavore picnic, where foods shared were grown and prepared locally, and also arrange town-wide garden tours while continuously promoting the message that resilience and sustainability must come from the ground up in the face of impending ecological crisis (J. Knapp-Cordes, personal communication, October 28, 2013).

Over the past four years, membership in the group has wavered, and Transition Framingham has attempted some programs and work groups that have failed to get off the ground. However, Knapp-Cordes and her fellow group members' resolve and commitment to reducing oil consumption and returning to a more local, natural, and communal lifestyle has remained steady. Their existing programs have become more popular and word has spread throughout the town about Transition Framingham and its goals. (J. Knapp-Cordes, personal communication, October 28, 2013).

Transition Framingham's mission and goals are steeped in the revitalization of the cultural commons. As part of the requirements of a course on current issues in adult environmental education, in the spring of 2014, I conducted ethnographic research. Through fieldwork, including interviews and observations during a garden tour, I sought to describe and interpret the shared patterns of values, behaviors, and beliefs of this particular culture-sharing group.

Transition Framingham and the Cultural Commons

A key characteristic of the cultural commons, decreasing dependency on a money economy and on consumerism while living in harmony with the

New Directions for Adult and Continuing Education • DOI: 10.1002/ace

natural world (Bowers, 2013), is evident in Transition Framingham. Bartering rather than money exchange is evident. For example, the group has a very popular seed-swapping program that allows individuals to trade seeds from their own garden for new ones to plant. No money is involved, and participants are able to share what they have while also getting new fruit and vegetable seeds that will ultimately be harvested for food.

In addition, skills or services swapped for other services is common practice. For example, rather than exchange fees, a high school student might be tutored in exchange for yard work (J. Knapp-Cordes, personal communication, October 28, 2013).

Less reliance of purchasing manufactured materials is highlighted. A tool-sharing system, for example, allows community members to borrow and swap home and gardening tools as needed, rather than having to buy new equipment thus decreasing demand for the manufacturing of new tools. Members of Transition Framingham also commit to less reliance on carbon emissions created through the use of automobiles. The group promotes biking as a form of transportation within the town and outlines safe biking routes during commuting hours.

Environmental awareness and conservation during the holidays is another example of the group's commitment to reduce consumption. "Greening the Holidays" is a program where the group runs workshops on how to move away from the consumer-driven, commercial-derived traditions of buying, waste, and excess and instead move toward handmade or recycled gifts, cards, wrapping, and decorations. The group holds intergenerational upcycled holiday craft events and vegan holiday cooking classes using locally sourced ingredients (J. Knapp-Cordes, personal communication, October 28, 2013).

Transition Framingham's commitment to mutual support systems and the sharing of intergenerational skills is also a hallmark of practice. One of the group's largest areas of interest, gardening, exemplifies the value of knowledge that is shared among peers or passed down from prior generations. The group organizes gardening tours that allow individuals to learn from their green-thumbed neighbors. Recipes are shared, techniques are modeled and explained, and canning workshops are held to preserve the harvest. During my research of the gardening practices, I witnessed older generations answering questions and offering guidance for newer enthusiasts. Those looking to get into gardening were eager for tips from their more experienced peers. In addition, some of the older members of the community are teaching younger generations how to sew and quilt (J. Knapp-Cordes, personal communication, October 28, 2013).

One critique of the movement to revitalize the cultural commons is that this requires one to abandon modern practices and revert to a time that existed long ago. Transition Framingham is an example of a community's ability to engender the commons in current times through small changes in daily practice. The community's environmental impact is lessened and a move toward nonmonetized exchanges, a more community-centered lifestyle, and the fostering of intergenerational knowledge and mutual support systems are all practices that do not require residents to revert to primitive times. By incorporating community learning relative to the revitalization of the cultural commons, residents can engender change.

The Transition Framingham group strives to promote the kind of lifelong learning that requires changes in previously established habits and activities in order to promote the types of resiliency and sustainability that are cornerstones of the cultural commons. Sharing knowledge among members is a component of both, and essential in creating new routines and lifestyles. Adult-learning theories are helpful lenses through which to examine the importance of knowledge sharing to influence change, as theories such as situated cognition, particularly the concepts of communities of practice and cognitive apprenticeships, prioritize this ideal.

More specifically, communities of practice, legitimate peripheral participation, and cognitive apprenticeships are lenses through which to view the cultural commons and Transition Framingham. These theories affirm the values of intergenerational knowledge and mentoring relationships that are critical cornerstones in both philosophies, while also acknowledging the importance of processes within work. Adult educators and individuals interested in affecting change through the revitalization of the commons can use these adult learning theories as ways to understand the effective means of knowledge sharing that can influence practices and ideologies at the community level.

Situated Learning, Cognitive Apprenticeships, and Communities of Practice

Situated learning is a theory of adult learning that posits that physical and social experiences are vital to the learning process and that knowledge cannot be evaluated separate from the situation in which the learning was presented (Merriam, Caffarella, & Baumgartner, 2007). According to situated learning theory, knowledge is gained through the process of participation and interaction with the community, the tools at hand, and activity.

Context is central to the learning that takes place in situated learning theory, as the context itself structures the learning (Merriam & Bierema, 2014). In situated learning theory, context is socially, culturally, and politically defined.

Situated learning theory is positioned in the constructivist learning paradigm, where it is believed that knowledge is socially constructed through experience and cannot be discovered but rather built and able to evolve throughout the learning process (Merriam & Bierema, 2014). In the constructivist orientation multiple realities exist, as there are many ways to obtain the same knowledge through different social constructions.

Situated learning theory has two central components (Lave & Wenger, 1991). The first element is the presence of a community of practice in which beliefs and behaviors are acquired in authentic contexts through social interaction and collaboration. In a community of practice, the learner develops knowledge through socialization, visualization, and imitation within a group of experienced individuals who share a craft, profession, or interest. However, communities of practice require more than just technical skill to complete a task. Rather, communities of practice are organized around a particular area of knowledge and give members a sense of collaboration and identity.

Transition Framingham is a community of practice that is centrally organized around the ideas of sustainability and resilience, governed by the principles of situated learning. Its core members serve as the experienced individuals who are leading community members toward a common goal using guided social avenues that allow participants to practice skills like gardening, composting, using locally sourced foods, and repairing tools, machines, and bicycles. It is a community-wide initiative that focuses on sharing knowledge socially through relationships.

The second critical piece of situated learning theory is legitimate peripheral participation during which the learner is given tasks on the periphery of the community of practice and, through experience, gradually increases responsibility and skill until he or she becomes an expert (Lave & Wenger, 1991). It is important to note that legitimate peripheral participation is more than just experiential learning, or learning by doing. Instead, legitimate peripheral participation positions individuals as full participants in the world and generators of meaning. For participants of Transition Framingham, legitimate peripheral participation occurs in many of the group's projects, but particularly in the community garden where newcomers are first invited to a community garden working group meeting to introduce interested parties to the basics of gardening. Following the informational meeting, new participants are able to shadow experienced gardeners and then cultivate their own plots within the community garden.

Cognitive apprenticeships are another type of situated cognition, and align with the values and goals of the cultural commons and the Transition Movement. The idea of cognitive apprenticeships, first attributed to Brown, Collins, and Duguid in 1989, acknowledges the ways that learning was accomplished through apprenticeships in earlier times. Just as the cultural commons and Transition Framingham value intergenerational knowledge and mentoring relationships, traditional apprenticeships used more experienced individuals to help learners observe the process, eventually assist, and finally work under the supervision of a mentor or guide.

Brown et al. (1989) used the idea of traditional physical apprenticeships and translated it to a more cerebral domain with the goal of making the teacher's thinking visible to the learner and the learner's thinking visible to the teacher by situating abstract tasks into authentic contexts. There are four dimensions to the cognitive apprenticeship framework that include content, method, sequence, and sociology. The first two dimensions, content and method, are central to the apprenticeship model and can be found in the cultural commons as well as in Transition Framingham.

New Directions for Adult and Continuing Education • DOI: 10.1002/ace

In the cognitive apprenticeship framework, the content dimension contains domain knowledge and heuristic strategies, which are effective techniques for accomplishing tasks that are considered "tricks of the trade" (Brown et al., 1989). The content dimension also houses control strategies, which are approaches used to control the way a task is carried out; and learning strategies, which are skills developed to extend, reconfigure, or apply learned skills to new problems or domains. In the cultural commons, these content strategies would be the tips and information shared across generations. In the Transition Movement, an example of the content dimension could be found within the gardening efforts. In Transition Framingham, a novice gardener was finally able to successfully grow corn after receiving a tip about organic soil fertilizer from an older gentleman in a neighboring plot.

The method dimension of cognitive apprenticeship focuses on the teaching methods used by the expert or guide (Brown et al., 1989). These methods include modeling, coaching, scaffolding, articulation, reflection, and exploration. During the modeling, coaching, and scaffolding phases, the expert gradually releases control and allows the student to slowly take on more responsibility. This is also seen in the mentoring components of both the cultural commons and Transition Framingham where knowledge is shared in a variety of ways, including having the expert perform a task so that the student can observe and build a conceptual model, allowing the expert to watch the student as he or she carries out the task while offering hints, feedback and reminders, and allowing the student the independence to try it on his or her own and return with questions.

Adult educators can pull from situated learning theory and the examples highlighted within the Transition Framingham Movement to create opportunities for knowledge sharing by seeking out experienced individuals to formally or informally educate others and fostering cognitive apprenticeships, while also promoting opportunities for legitimate peripheral participation. Adult educators may initially need to facilitate social connections that introduce individuals to the talents and expertise that reside within other community members, and even explicitly outline the benefits of revitalizing the commons. However, the structure of communities of practice and cognitive apprenticeships allows for participants to gradually take ownership over their own practices within a supportive community environment.

Conclusion

The Transition Movement and the cultural commons both recognize the interconnectedness of all entities in an ecosystem, and the responsibility to share that knowledge with others in ways that promote nonmonetized economies and a smaller ecological footprint. Situated learning theory, specifically communities of practice, legitimate peripheral participation and cognitive apprenticeships are constructs through which to view these shared values as these adult learning theories highlight the importance of the same mentoring relationships and intergenerational knowledge that are found in both the Transition Movement and the cultural commons. Transition Framingham seeks a community-centered lifestyle that is in harmony with the natural world as a means to forging societies that are more resilient and sustainable in a time of an unpredictable and environmentally unstable future.

References

Bowers, C. A. (2013). *In the grip of the past: Educational reforms that address what should be changed and what should be conserved.* Eugene, OR: Eco-Justice Press.

Bowers, C. A. (2009). Educating for a revitalization of the cultural commons. *Canadian Journal of Environmental Education, 14,* 196–200.

Brookfield, S. (1984). The contribution of Eduard Lindeman to the development of theory and philosophy in adult education. *Adult Education Quarterly, 34*(4), 185–196.

Brown, J. S., Collins, A., & Duguid, P. (1989). Situated cognition and the culture of learning. *Educational Researcher, 18*(1), 32–42.

Business Alliance for Local Living Economies. (2012). *Why we do this work.* Retrieved from https://bealocalist.org/why_we_work

Hopkins, R. (2008). *The transition handbook: From oil dependency to local resilience.* Devon, UK: Green Books.

Hopkins, R., & Lipman, P. (2009). *Who we are and what we do.* Retrieved from http://www.transitionnetwork.org/resources/who-we-are-and-what-we-do

Lave, J., & Wenger, E. (1991). *Situated learning: Legitimate peripheral participation.* Cambridge, UK: Cambridge University.

Lindeman, E. C. (1937). Introduction. In T.K. Brown (Ed.), *Adult education for social change.* Philadelphia, PA: Swarthmore Seminar.

McMichael, A. (2013). Globalization, climate change, and human health. *New England Journal of Medicine, 368,* 1335–1343.

Merriam, S. B., & Bierema, L. L. (2014). *Adult learning: Linking theory and practice.* San Francisco, CA: Jossey-Bass.

Merriam, S. B., Caffarella, R. S., & Baumgartner, L. (2007). *Learning in adulthood: A comprehensive guide* (3rd ed.). San Francisco, CA: Jossey-Bass.

Norberg-Hodge, H. (2010). *The economics of happiness.* Retrieved from http://countercurrents.org

United States Environmental Protection Agency. (2013). *Climate change.* Retrieved from http://www3.epa.gov/climatechange

EMILY KEARNS BURKE *is a public school teacher within the Framingham Public Schools of Massachusetts.*

New Directions for Adult and Continuing Education • DOI: 10.1002/ace

INDEX